LEADERSHIP

by

THE BOOK

*Lessons from
Every Book of the Bible*

Brent Garrison

elevate
faith

Endorsements

"I enjoyed reading *Leadership by the Book* by my friend, Brent Garrison. A challenge, an insight, a Biblical perspective, a role model and sometimes a good old kick in the pants. As a leader, being regularly encouraged with a Biblical model for leaders is powerful and centering. I hope you find as much value from these leadership lessons as I have."

Dr. Pat Gelsinger, CEO VMware

"Brent Garrison has accomplished an enormous feat. He has undertaken a panoramic survey of the entire Bible and uncovered leadership nuggets from every book. Drawing upon his extensive background in training leaders at all levels, he provides a delightful, encouraging, and inspiring resource that you will use over and over again."

Dr. Richard Blackaby, *Spiritual Leadership* and *The Inspired Leader*

"You will enjoy and learn from this book! Based on insights God has provided through His Word, Brent has captured many leadership principles that others have missed. It is written in a style to allow you to use as a devotional (which I have done and recommend), but you will not want to wait to read all of the 66 insightful chapters. Each chapter is extremely well written making it a delightful read for all."

Dean Borgman, CEO Sikorsky Helicopter, retired

"Brent Garrison knows that without leadership, nothing happens. Nothing. So, we should not be surprised that there are insights about leadership all through the Bible. Brent helps all of us by going through the various Bible books to find insights to help us see leadership from various perspectives. These nuggets will help all of us realize that there are different kinds of leaders and different challenges, but God is there to help us rise to the task. Thanks, Brent, for giving us a new way at looking at leadership!"

Dr. Erwin W. Lutzer, Moody Church, Chicago

"Communities and businesses the world over have grown weary of ineffective, self-serving leaders. Brent Garrison draws authentic and profound insights on 'leadership that works' from God Himself. His practical and 'bite-sized' insights make this a great tool for anyone who wants to be a selfless, more effective leader in their unique circle of influence."

Mark W. Albers, Senior Vice President Exxon Mobil Corporation

"I have known Brent for many years, as he has demonstrated real leadership at three colleges we've been involved with at PING. We've seen firsthand how Christian-based principles, illuminated by Scripture, can bring clarity and positive change. With this important book, Brent delivers refreshing and timeless message that will inspire not only today's leaders but tomorrow's as well."

Allan Solheim, Executive Vice President, retired, PING

"What a great idea Brent Garrison has come up with. He has given us a leadership lesson from every book of the Bible! I love how Brent has researched God's Word for teaching Christian leaders how we can improve our leadership. I recommend you use this great tool as a daily devotional for upgrading your service to others in leadership."

Dr. Hans Finzel, President of HDLeaders and
author of *The Top Ten Mistakes Leaders Make* (David C Cook)

"Dr. Brent Garrison has written a powerful book that shows why the Bible is the ultimate leadership resource. In each thought-provoking chapter—one for each book of the Bible—he connects the dots between character, leadership, and God's Word. Whether you head up a small organization or a Fortune 500 corporation, you will find the lessons in this book to be timely, meaningful, and easy to implement. Keep it close by your desk, because you'll want to refer to it again and again."

Mac McQuiston, CEO, CEO Forum

"Leadership is about wisdom, judgement, serving and vision. What better place to learn about these qualities then from their Originator? *Leadership by The Book* puts the foundation of leadership front and center, and guides the reader to look at God's Word from the perspective of what each book has to say to His followers about leading from the perspective of eternity."

Rich McClure, former President, UniGroup, Inc.
(Parent of United Van Lines and Mayflower Transit)

"Leadership by The Book is a 'must read' for those seeking God's leadership for their organizations. The truth of God's Word strengthens our hearts and resolve and takes us to places beyond which we could ask for or even imagine. Worry, panic and dread are replaced by the thrill of a roller coaster ride when you know, beyond all doubt, that God's in charge and everyone watching is being drawn closer to Him."

Barry Meguiar, Meguiar's Care Care and host of Car Crazy television

"After having had the privilege to be in leadership positions throughout my life I don't consider myself an expert but I am always cautious about 'another book on leadership.' If you hold that same view, I strongly encourage you to throw that caution to the wind in favor of this book. Brent has carefully captured leadership from God's perspective in a most applicable manner. Focused but information filled chapters end with a very comfortable application that is ready for any reader to use. Yes, read this one!"

Patrick P Caruana Lt. Gen. (RET) USAF

"Books about leadership abound, but *Leadership by The Book* looks to the Bible for its inspiration. Since my personal faith is so important to me I enjoyed this leadership resource since it seeks to look at leadership through God's eyes. There are some leaders who prefer to lead only through this world's mindset, so be prepared to be challenged by reading this book to consider a different perspective, one of humility and a servant's heart—Christ's example."

Jerry Colangelo, USA Basketball

"Brent Garrison's *Leadership by The Book* is a profoundly useful book for all leaders who want to be effective at leading and also effective at integrating scriptural truth in how they lead. Garrison masterfully writes about leadership principles from every book of the Bible and draws out seminal truths that will guide us to being great leaders. Brent Garrison is an outstanding educator who designed the format of the book so that we will actually learn something, a rare gift in today's book world. Move *Leadership by The Book* to the top of the stack!"

Dr. Tim Irwin, *New York Times* Best Selling Author and Speaker

"Dr. Brent Garrison, once a colleague, now a friend, is a born leader. But never content to coast on his innate ability to show the way, he is ever curious, constantly challenging, studying, searching to move from good to better to best. In *Leadership by The Book*, he has reached a pinnacle, pointing leaders to the ultimate source of inspiration where one learns to lead the pack—from the back."

Jerry B. Jenkins, Multiple *New York Times* Bestselling Author

Editorial Work: Anna McHargue and Dave Troesh

Cover Design: Arthur Cherry

Interior Layout: Leslie Hertling

Published in Boise, Idaho by Elevate Faith, a division of Elevate Publishing.

www.elevatepub.com

For information please email: info@elevatepub.com.

ISBN (print): 9781943425020

Library of Congress: 2015917867

Printed in the United States of America

Dedication

Since this is a book about leadership from a Biblical perspective I must begin by mentioning the person who invited me to a church camp where I met my Savior. It was at this camp my faith journey began over four decades ago. Bill Peterson was my neighbor growing up in Northwest Indiana and my best friend and brother for many years until his untimely death.

Next, to the leader who hired me for my first assignment in education, Denny Brown. Denny was not only the principal at the Christian high school where I taught science, but became a great friend and mentor in leadership.

Dr. Howard Whaley, another leadership mentor during my years at Moody Bible Institute. Howard is a life-long learner and asked the same of those who reported to him. He constantly challenged me to become a better leader and that the Scriptures serve as a huge part of that process.

Two other men who had profound impact in my leadership development were Jim Tulloch and Dean Borgman. During my 15 years as president of a Christian college they served as board chairmen and were a constant encouragement, support, and leadership example. I can't thank these men enough for their investment in my life.

Mac McQuiston, founder and CEO of CEO Forum must also be on my dedication list by allowing me the honor of joining CEO Forum over 5 years ago and the opportunity to minister to Christian business leaders.

Finally, Maggi, my bride of over 40 years, who has been my sounding board, constant support through the ups and downs of leadership assignments, and painfully honest when needed.

I'm deeply grateful to those mentioned in this dedication, and to others who have been an example of biblical leadership.

Foreword

As a leader, I often ask the question, "What's the most important thing in leadership?" My answer always starts with a reference to character. While many leadership books and seminars offer helpful suggestions about how to get things done as a leader, my concern is about who you are as you lead. Outcomes are achievable without character, even jaw dropping outcomes. But if the process to produce the outcomes is compromised by a lack of character then the outcomes will ultimately be tainted and the people who compromise integrity for gain become tainted as well. Leadership without character may change your bottom line but it will also change the leader for a net loss.

The sink hole of leadership without character was made dramatically evident when the U.S. Environmental Protection agency reported that Volkswagen covered up an emissions issue with millions of its diesel engines. I have tried to envision the boardroom at Volkswagen when the news hit that the car's engine design didn't meet stringent emission standards. *The New York Times* reported that Volkswagen created an engine management program, which would allow an engine to pass emission testing, but turn itself off after testing to allow better mileage and power to meet customer expectations. This fix allowed the cars to pass inspection, but when deactivated caused the diesel engine to emit 40 times more pollution than standards allow! The problem was more than tainted air… it was tainted people who led simply for the outcomes.

Leadership by The Book: Lessons from Every Book of the Bible seeks to challenge leaders – all leaders – to consider a leadership style that embraces the rich outcomes of character-led leadership. Brent's book effectively motivates and inspires us to align our practice with the leadership principles that are found in the timeless wisdom of Scripture. The temptation for leaders to make decisions that transgress the wisdom of God's Word for personal gain or glory are many. But the outcome of these decisions is predictable, as demonstrated by decisions made by leaders at Volkswagen. The former CEO resigned in disgrace, and the financial fallout will be in the billions.

This is not just like any other book on leadership. Not only is its content full of unique perspectives, but it is also unique in that it is written in small chapters, one for every book of the Bible, which makes it useful as a leadership devotional or a basis for discussions with other leaders. Brent also encourages readers to keep a leadership journal as they consider various reflections on leading, which in turn will help personalize the concepts of this book into practical action steps.

I know Brent's heart and his passion for Biblical leadership. It shows on every page! May his prayer that this book challenge you to lead differently, and, in fact, as Christ led, be answered in your life as you read.

Dr. Joseph Stowell, past president of Moody Bible Institute, president of Cornerstone University

Table of Contents

Introduction

*Leadership by The Book:
Lessons From Every Book of The Bible.*

Why Another Book About Leadership?
Do we really need another book on leadership? After all, there are over 166,000 books about leadership listed in Amazon, so the question certainly is appropriate.

I'd like to suggest that this book is different from other books about leadership for several reasons:

- A lesson on leadership from each of the 66 books of the Bible demonstrates the Bible is a significant resource for leadership.

- 66 bite-sized chapters which can be read quickly, used for personal devotion or while discussing leadership with others.

- Designed to be read along with a journal for reflection. Without the "so what?" we are simply reading a book without driving its concepts deeper into our hearts and minds.

Most books about leadership are written from <u>our</u> perspective, as the created. I wanted to write a book about leadership, which gave the prominent role to the Creator and <u>His</u> thoughts about leadership. After all, since we are created by God, there is no one who better understands our heart, our motives, our nature and our abilities. God could be described as the CEO of the Universe and the greatest leader ever imagined; His Son, Jesus Christ, manifested this same nature through His leadership during His time on earth.

Think about this, even though Jesus never held a position of formal leadership and only led a small, motley group, His life had more impact than any other leader in history! I don't know about you, but as a leader, I want to know more about that kind of leadership and the character He had to lead such an impactful life.

My desire, in writing this book, is for you to view the Bible as the greatest leadership resource in your library and for you to be driven to know the Creator in a deeper way, for He wants every leader to tap into the truth of Scripture.

Leadership is about making good decisions and executing them well. But, it cannot be separated from character, for character is the way we treat one another. God created mankind in His image, therefore, mankind is the most important aspect of life. All too often, leaders view people as a means to an end rather than the end itself—the purpose for your leadership is to relate to others with character.

Reflection

If you don't have a journal, you quickly will discover that you will benefit from one while reading this book, especially at the end of each chapter where you will find leadership reflection questions. Please use this section to consider the lesson topic and record your thoughts in the journal. I believe some very important ideas will be revealed as you reflect about leadership. Don't simply read this book without reflecting, then you have done nothing more than read another book about leadership. I desire that you are transformed into a true Biblical leader, who not only knows Biblical concepts, but also applies them.

Since the chapters are short, they don't take much time to review, so you might consider using each chapter as a leadership devotional or as a leadership discussion starter. As a leader you have those who report to you, so why not initiate conversations about leadership. Also, although each chapter begins with a passage from Scripture, I believe a person unfamiliar with the Bible will still easily gain leadership insights from each lesson.

May God use the Bible and this resource to help you become a leader of passion, skill and character (Romans 12:8).

#1: GENESIS

Joe's Life as a Leader

My purpose in writing *Leadership by The Book: Lessons From Every Book of the Bible* is to help you see God's Word as an incredible resource for leadership training. God peppers stories about leaders throughout the Scriptures for us to learn from—their successes and failures. Stories are powerful tools to envision a principle in a way that is memorable and personal. This is why case studies are so popular in business schools. They put flesh to the topic being taught. I trust you will enjoy this first of 66 lessons, for in it, we have one of the best.

Genesis 37-50 NLT

- *Now Israel loved Joseph more than any of his other sons. (37:3)*

- *Joseph had a dream. (37:5)*

- *"Come, let's sell him to the Ishmaelites." (37:27)*

- *The LORD was with Joseph and he prospered. (39:2)*

- *"My master has withheld nothing from me except you, because you are his wife. How then could I do such a wicked thing and sin against God?" (39:9)*

- *But while Joseph was there in the prison, the LORD was with him. (39:20b-21a)*

- *"But when all goes well with you, remember me and show me kindness: Mention me to Pharaoh and get me out of this prison." (Genesis 40:14)*

- *The chief cupbearer, however, did not remember Joseph; he forgot him. (40:23)*

- *"I cannot do it," Joseph replied to Pharaoh, "but God will give Pharaoh the answer he desires." (41:16)*

- *"There is no one so discerning and wise as you—only with respect to the throne will I be greater than you."* (41:39, 40)

- *"Do not be angry with yourselves for selling me here, because it was to save lives that God sent me ahead of you."* (45:5) NIV

If you haven't already, take time to read the section in Genesis which deals with Joseph (chapters 37-50). Joseph is my favorite leader in Scripture (other than our Lord). His story about a dysfunctional family, shows the ebb and flow of personal circumstances, and depicts a man who lived above the fray when wronged.

The cited Scriptures provide a glimpse into what people thought about this man. He certainly elicited strong feelings from those who knew him. His father loved him most, but his brothers hated him; Potiphar loved him for how he ran his home, but wanted to placate his wife; his prison mates could go either way (one loved him and one hated his vision); Pharaoh was amazed at his skills of dream interpretation and noticed his wisdom; and his brothers were terrified of him when they found out he ruled over much of Egypt.

Joseph was a leader's leader! How many men, when found in the circumstances he faced, would react as he did? Probably none, for most of us would react with anger and a pity party. Theologians see a type of Christ in Joseph and I think they are right. Here we have a man wronged in unimaginable ways who showed no guile toward those who mistreated him. Also, he was placed (supernaturally, I might add) in a position that allowed him to protect his family members, who would become a nation of promise through his effective leadership. Finally, he understood (Genesis 45:5—*do not be angry with yourselves for selling me here, because it was to save lives that God sent me ahead of you.*) that his sufferings were designed for a higher purpose than the here and now.

So what do you take away from Joe's life? We can learn a lot about how to lead with Christlikeness through Joseph's story. Following are some questions that hopefully whet your appetite to lead with a better understanding of what made Joseph a unique leader.

Reflections on Leadership:

This is your first leadership reflection section so please get your journal and work through the following questions. Reading about leadership is important, but how much more valuable is it when you consider and apply what you are learning. My prayer is that your journal becomes a place where God's Spirit speaks to your heart and mind to help you be a better leader. Those being led deserve leaders who reflect their faith, not just talk about it.

1. Have you ever worked in a situation where a colleague was favored? How did that impact the way you led or followed?

2. Think back to a situation where you were misunderstood, wronged, passed over, or just challenged.

    •   Were you able to grow from those circumstances or did they embitter you?

    •   How does the Bible ask us to live when circumstances are less than desirable?

3. Leadership is all about relationships. Joseph had those who loved and hated him.

    •   How did Joseph react to those who hated him?

    •   What principles can you identify that Joseph used in dealing with difficult situations?

    •   Does the Bible have anything to say about how we treat those who wrong us?

4. Consider the following quotes about being wronged and reflect how they apply to your leading.

   - *"The work that God does in us when we wait is usually more important than the thing for which we wait!"* Erwin W. Lutzer, *When You've Been Wronged: Moving From Bitterness to Forgiveness*

   - *"Anger dwells only in the bosom of fools."* Albert Einstein

#2: EXODUS

Between a Rock and a Hard Place

The whole Israelite community set out from the Desert of Sin, traveling from place to place as the Lord commanded. They camped at Rephidim, but there was no water for the people to drink. So they quarreled with Moses and said, "Give us water to drink."

Moses replied, "Why do you quarrel with me? Why do you put the LORD to the test?"

But the people were thirsty for water there, and they grumbled against Moses. They said, "Why did you bring us up out of Egypt to make us and our children and livestock die of thirst?"

Then Moses cried out to the LORD, "What am I to do with these people? They are almost ready to stone me."

The LORD answered Moses, "Go out in front of the people. Take with you some of the elders of Israel and take in your hand the staff with which you struck the Nile, and go. I will stand there before you by the rock at Horeb. Strike the rock, and water will come out of it for the people to drink." So Moses did this in the sight of the elders of Israel. And he called the place Massah and Meribah because the Israelites quarreled and because they tested the LORD saying, "Is the LORD among us or not?" (17:1-7)

Our second leadership story is about Moses, a leader between a rock and a hard place. Let's examine Moses' reaction to a most challenging leadership scenario—lack of water. Since I live in a desert climate, I know something about how these people must have felt, thinking they were going to die of thirst. However, if we think about the Exile story, it is abundantly clear that God wasn't going to allow the Israelites to die of dehydration since He had already provided for their welfare in miraculous ways. Therefore, the problem wasn't water, but trust and patience. Trust that God would again provide for their needs (e.g. manna, quail, pillar of fire or smoke, shoes that didn't wear out, etc.), and patience with the timing of His provision.

As a leader, you have had those situations where board members, direct reports and employees have come to you with their frustrations. Here, Moses was fully aware of the need for water; he must have been parched as well. I'm sure he was frustrated with the situation, but when they approached him with complaints he did two things: one, he shifted blame; and two, he reminded them that they shouldn't put God to the test (Deuteronomy 6:16).

I might be reading too much into his comment, *"Why do you quarrel with me?"*, but there are other responses that Moses could have used to show leadership rather than deflecting the blame. His second response in this story tells us a bit more about his leadership mindset, *"What am I to do with these people?"* Moses was extremely frustrated with the people he was called to lead—can you relate? In fact, he was a broken leader by the time he faces a similar situation in Numbers 20. He had just lost his sister and now this generation was testing God, just like the previous one.

One of those higher standards in leadership is accepting responsibility. Yes, even when the situation isn't of your doing. Blame shifting isn't leadership and it isn't what people need from leaders when facing challenges. We all know about Harry Truman's desk sign, "The Buck Stops Here!" In his farewell address to the American people he stated, "The President—whoever he is—has to decide. He can't pass the buck to anybody. No one else can do the deciding for him. That's his job." Leadership acts. It does not shift the blame.

God picked the stories we have in Scripture for a purpose—to teach. Moses' leadership assignment was unique in all of history. All leaders have something in common with Moses—complaining people and feeling alone at the top. The following questions are designed to remind us of our responsibility as leaders and especially as Christlike leaders.

Reflections on Leadership:

1. Haven't we all shifted blame as leaders? I know I have and am ashamed when I do.

    • How do you feel when someone in leadership shifts the blame and why does it elicit this response?

    • Have you ever considered the idea that Christ could have shifted the blame for our sins and told the Father we aren't worthy of redeeming? Journal about this idea of Christ's willingness to take the blame for our sins.

2. Fed up with those you lead? If you lead, you have felt this frustration.

    • Are you frustrated with those you lead right now? Can you imagine how Christ felt with the motley crew He interacted with? During the next week review the Gospels and mark those sections of Scripture where the disciples frustrated Christ. Note how He dealt with them.

    • Take the list you just made and consider how Christ's example of dealing with difficult colleagues might be put into your box of leadership tools to better handle future leadership frustrations.

3. Read the following quotes about frustration and make application to your leadership.

    • *"I've come to believe that all my past failure and frustration were actually laying the foundation for the understandings that have created the new level of living I now enjoy."* Tony Robbins

    • *"Our fatigue is often caused not by work, but by worry, frustration and resentment."* Dale Carnegie

#3: LEVITICUS

I Didn't Know

When a leader sins <u>unintentionally</u> and does what is forbidden in any of the commands of the LORD his God, when he realizes his guilt and the sin he has committed becomes known, he must bring as his offering a male goat without defect. He is to lay his hand on the goat's head and slaughter it at the place where the burnt offering is slaughtered before the LORD. It is a sin offering. Then the priest shall take some of the blood of the sin offering with his finger and put it on the horns of the altar of burnt offering and pour out the rest of the blood at the base of the altar. He shall burn all the fat on the altar as he burned the fat of the fellowship offering. In this way the priest will make atonement for the leader's sin, and he will be forgiven. (4:22-26)

The operative word in this passage is *unintentionally*. This word is used several times in this chapter and, in Hebrew, means to sin in ignorance. Context is important here as this Scripture passage deals with the giving of Levitical Law and all of its specificity. We live in a very different economy of grace today, yet the New Testament outlines details on how we are to think, speak and live. Even with all the instructions on how to live in the Bible, it is likely we will commit sins without our knowing (in ignorance).

As a leader, you don't get the luxury of living a private life, so your sins are "out there" for all to see. Somehow your unintentional sin comes to light. This sin could be either one of omission (something you should have done) or commission (wrong action or attitude). It's difficult enough for a Christian to admit they sinned, but this is exacerbated for a leader. I know you will agree that one of the challenges of leadership is keeping pride in check, especially when those who report to us notice something less than admirable about our attitude or actions.

Since unintentional sin is committed in ignorance, it probably comes to light through someone else mentioning it. You then have the conundrum of either accepting their perspective or thinking, "That's your take, but not mine." or "Do you know who you are talking to?"

I accept my sin more readily when I realize it rather than when another brings it to my attention. Yet, Biblical leaders must be open to what others see in their leadership and demonstrate a teachable and humble spirit—remember the mind-of-Christ examples of humility and servitude from Philippians 2. This Christlike mindset is the opposite of how many leaders react when their foibles are exposed. "I'm the leader and I don't need you calling out my shortcomings." Dr. Tim Irwin's book, *Derailed*, tells how six leaders were derailed because of the hubris that can overtake a leader in the rarified air of a CEO's office.

Sin is an old-fashioned idea and certainly not a notion in today's business world, but as Christians, we understand its significance. Aren't we blessed that we don't have to obtain a goat's blood for temporary redemption? Our permanent redemption comes from the matchless work of our Savior's death on the cross.

Remember, we are talking about unintentional sin and not preferences that others might expect of you. The Church has a problem explaining this difference, so don't be surprised when the world doesn't understand the difference between sins and preferences. Sins are those actions or attitudes that God deems are wrong where preferences are man's list of what he believes to be wrong. As a leader, you need to think through this issue or you will try to please everyone or become so hardened you try to please only yourself. Ricky Nelson's song, *Garden Party* has a line in it about not being able to please everyone, so you've got to please yourself. The song did well on the charts, but contains lousy theology. Our goal is to please the Father. In doing this, we will do well in life.

Since Christ's work is complete, when we confess our sins, we know we have forgiveness and a renewed relationship to the Father through Christ. However, we have a responsibility to make our sin right with those we've wronged. Making it right is often tough. Accepting correction from another is hard, but making it right can be even more difficult. However, a leader who admits a wrong and makes amends is one who will instill a higher sense of loyalty from those they lead.

Reflections on Leadership:

1. Have you ever had another confront you about something in your life?

    •   If so, what was the situation and what sin did you commit? What was your reaction to the person who confronted you?

    •   Was the confrontation about a sin or a preference of the other person? If it wasn't about sin, how did you help the other person understand the difference?

2. Do you struggle as a leader having others confront you about words or actions? Consider your reaction when others confront you to ensure that your reaction aligns with Scripture.

3. Read the following quotes about accountability and reflect in your journal how it applies to you.

    •   *"A body of men holding themselves accountable to nobody ought not to be trusted by anybody."* Thomas Paine

    •   *"Ninety-nine percent of all failures come from people who have a habit of making excuses."* George Washington Carver

#4: NUMBERS

Share the Leadership Load

Moses said to the LORD, <u>"Why are you treating me, your servant, so harshly?</u> Have mercy on me! What did I do to deserve the burden of all these people? Did I give birth to them? Did I bring them into the world? Why did you tell me to carry them in my arms like a mother carries a nursing baby? How can I carry them to the land you swore to give their ancestors? Where am I supposed to get meat for all these people? They keep whining to me, saying, 'Give us meat to eat!' I can't carry all these people by myself! <u>The load is far too heavy! If this is how you intend to treat me, just go ahead and kill me.</u> Do me a favor and spare me this misery!"

Then the LORD said to Moses, "Gather before me seventy men who are recognized as elders and leaders of Israel. Bring them to the Tabernacle to stand there with you. I will come down and talk to you there. <u>I will take some of the Spirit that is upon you, and I will put the Spirit upon them also. They will bear the burden of the people along with you, so you won't have to carry it alone.</u>" (11:11-17) NLT

Ever feel like Moses? The burden of leadership is too much; the people I lead are like babies; and the challenges are overwhelming! Welcome to the world of leadership. If you are a leader, you have had feelings that mirror those of Moses.

Let's face it, the life of a leader has its perks, but it also has its downside. Having held various leadership positions in higher education, I have come to the conclusion that a leader has two main responsibilities. First, to serve as the catalyst of vision—a catalyst is a chemical added to a formula to determine the direction and speed of a chemical reaction. So too, a leader crafts a vision and then assembles the resources to accomplish it. Second, a leader must assemble a team to share the burden of leadership.

We all know them. Leaders who believe they are the only ones who can do it right, or fail to delegate to other capable individuals. I've also seen leaders who were intimidated or jealous of those who demonstrated greater leadership skills than they. Leaders must understand they multiply leadership effectiveness by sharing leadership with others. If another leader on your team shows great promise and you encourage their growth, you will probably get the credit for their work as well as strengthen the leadership foundation of the company. Remember, you were that young leader once and someone invested in you to help you become the leader you are today.

Moses whined about his leadership assignment, so God responded by asking him to gather 70 leaders to spread the leadership burden. You probably remember that Moses' father-in-law, Jethro, suggested a "share the load" approach in Exodus 18:1-27. Here, Moses was overwhelmed by judging all the cases brought before him. He became a leadership bottleneck by handling everything himself, thus failing to serve those he was called to lead. Theodore Roosevelt says it best; "The best executive is the one who has sense enough to pick good men to do what he wants done, and self-restraint enough to keep from meddling with them while they do it."

If you are a leader who has difficulties sharing the load you must learn to do so, for by sharing the load you multiply yourself and encourage others. Don't let leadership pride convince you that you are the only one who can do it right or you will drive good leaders from your organization by ignoring their abilities. Plus, by sharing the load with others you will be able to work on balance in your life.

Reflections on Leadership:

1. Leadership burden: Do you feel the burden of leadership right now? If so, what is causing the burden (people, decisions or challenges)? This passage reminds leaders that they need to share the burden, so how are you doing with sharing yours? Make a journal entry concerning this question of the burden of leadership.

2. Growing leaders: Delegation is a skill that every leader must develop. Interact with the following questions:

    *   Are you looking for potential leaders in your company? Think back to your early years as a leader and remember how others helped you become the leader you are today.

    *   Evaluate your leadership team and ask the following:

        *   Do I have the right members in the team to enable the company to be effective? If not, what needs to change to create the best team?

        *   Do you actively select, evaluate, confront and train your team or do you leave this responsibility to others?

3. Review the following quotes about developing leaders.

    *   *"Leaders don't create followers, they create more leaders."* Tom Peters

    *   *"Leaders aren't born, they are made. And they are made just like anything else, through hard work. And that's the price we'll have to pay to achieve that goal, or any goal."* Vince Lombardi

#5: DEUTERONOMY

Boiling 10 Down to 1

1. *You shall have no other gods before me.*

2. *You shall not make for yourself an idol in the form of anything in heaven above or on the earth.*

3. *You shall not misuse the name of the LORD your God.*

4. *Observe the Sabbath day by keeping it holy.*

5. *Honor your father and mother.*

6. *You shall not murder.*

7. *You shall not commit adultery.*

8. *You shall not steal.*

9. *You shall not give false testimony.*

10. *You shall not covet your neighbor's wife . . . or anything that belongs to your neighbor.* (5:7-21)

The Ten Commandments or Decalogue are located in Exodus 20 and here in Deuteronomy 5. Today, this list is perceived as antiquated, but in reality they are as timely now as when they were given. This God-given list is proof that keeping a mere 10 commands is impossible, especially when the New Testament added another level of adherence, that if we even *think* about a sin, we are guilty.

Boiling Things Down

I like simple things. If you think about it, the theme of Scripture is *relationship*. We were created to relate to our God, our sin broke that relationship and this broken relationship is renewed in Christ. The Ten Commandments can likewise be boiled down to one theme: *stealing.*

Take each of the commands and look at it through the lens of something stolen: stealing God's glory, stealing His name, stealing a day, stealing a life and so on. Taking something that doesn't belong to you breaks the heart of God and brings judgment on the perpetrator.

This leadership lesson is a reminder of how we are to live as people of faith. Leader or not, we are to conduct our lives in a way that shows respect and honor for others. However, a leader is called to a higher level of responsibility, competency, attitude and actions. As a leader, you are constantly challenged to remember who is in charge. By the way, it's not you. You have the title, but God's name and sovereignty trump any title you have.

Leaders can also rationalize working every day of the week. Some forget that rest was designed by God to give us an opportunity to reflect on Him and to renew our bodies. The pressure-cooker environment of business can challenge our integrity with the temptation to cook financials, represent a situation in our favor or cutting costs at the employee's expense. You might also face the temptation of entering into an inappropriate relationship that comes as part of that power and position.

The Ten Commandments are God's Big 10 List. David Letterman has used the Top 10 List for decades, but his list isn't dealing with eternal or critically important subjects. God's list must also be understood in the context of relationship. The list is about stealing, but it is also about relating to God and others. Notice that the first four commands are how we relate to God and the final six how we relate to others. There is no mistaking the fact that if our relationship with God is weak or non-existent, we will treat others inappropriately. Conversely, as we live in proximity to the Father, we treat others with honor and love.

This vertical and horizontal relationship is seen clearly in the dialog between the young lawyer and Jesus in Matthew 22:34-40 in his question, *"Which is the greatest commandment in the Law?"* Christ's answer is a reference to the Ten

Commandments since they lay out God's intent for His Creation. The only component of Creation that can relate to God is mankind. Therefore, God designed the plan of redemption to correct a destroyed relationship because of our sin. Christ's passion was to complete the task of reconciling us to the Father so we could again live in relationship with Him.

Leadership is about relationship, since a leader can only accomplish goals through the interaction of people living in relationship. Therefore, the way you live your life has a profound impact not only on those who relate to you, but to the entity you lead. Reflection on the following questions will help you evaluate how you are keeping the commandments and aligning yourself with God's design in relationship.

Reflections on Leadership:

1. Stealing: Take your journal and reflect on the following questions:

    •   Are you working too many days and hours because you need to or because work is easy compared to dealing with other aspects of life (e.g. family or faith)? Are you pleased with the time or priority you give your faith? If not, why have you allowed your faith to take a back seat, and how does this impact your life?

    •   If you are working too much, set up a time when you can discuss this issue with your spouse. Be transparent about this issue since gaining balance in time management is critical. Life is comprised of time, talent and treasure, so how you use time is of great importance.

2. Relationship: How we live in relationship is what life is all about. How we live in relationship to God determines how we will live with others. Be honest with this question: Are you aligned with God by giving that relationship its due, and if not, what needs to change to correct this critical issue?

    •   Evaluate the way you treat others. Are you pleased with family relations? Does your spouse know your love for God and for him or her? Do your children see your faith lived out in your life, or do they see duplicity? Where shortcomings are evident, how will you make corrections?

3. Review the following quotes about God's commands for your application.

    •   *"It comes down to the Ten Commandments. They weren't ten suggestions. They were Ten Commandments."* Donny Osmond

    •   *"This man's spiritual power has been precisely this, that he has distinguished between custom and creed. He has broken the conventions, but he has kept the commandments."* G.K. Chesterton

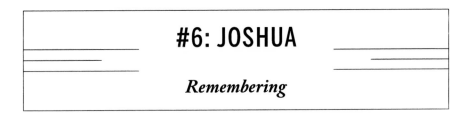

#6: JOSHUA

Remembering

So Joshua called together the twelve men he had appointed from the Israelites, one from each tribe, and said to them, "Go over before the ark of the LORD your God into the middle of the Jordon. Each of you is to take up a stone on his shoulder, according to the number of the tribes of the Israelites, to serve as a sign among you." (4:4-6a)

There are two books in the Bible replete with stories and principles on leadership: Joshua and Nehemiah.

In the book of Joshua, two Scriptures come to mind: Joshua 1:8, where keeping the Law leads to prosperous and successful living; and Joshua 24:15, where we see leadership at its finest through Joshua's challenge, *"As for me and my household, we will serve the LORD."* Our leadership story from Joshua is about remembering. God commanded Joshua, after they crossed the Jordon River into the Promised Land, to erect a pillar (Ebenezer) to remember what He did in bringing them to the land flowing with milk and honey.

God knows that it is easy for us to forget His mighty works. Therefore, He created mnemonic devices to help us remember.

- Baptism is a symbol of dying to the old life and alive to a new life (Romans 6)

- Remembering Christ's death through Communion (1 Corinthians 11)

- Israel's Seven Feasts to celebrate God's faithfulness to this nation (Leviticus 23)

- Stone monuments after entering the Promised Land to commemorate God's protection in their wanderings (Joshua 4)

- Phylacteries in Deuteronomy 6:4-9 which were to help Israel remember God's faithfulness

Leaders need to learn the importance of remembering as well. They can lead a company or ministry to great accomplishments yet have those events forgotten, almost overnight.

It's frustrating, but is often the reality when working with people. The old adage is true: "What have you done for me today?" may be what most people think about your leadership in the same way you remember their successes. Far too often though, we only remember their failures. During seminary, I sold Fords and each month's sales were marked on a board in the sales manager's office. You might have been the top salesman one month, but it was a whole new game the next; so too, we can lead with this mindset.

Books and articles about leadership often overlook the importance of remembering. Vision is always mentioned since it maps out the future, but remembering the accomplishments of the past are important as well, because remembering helps put the present and future in context.

Remembrance events should highlight the past and recall the milestones that made the company great as well as cast a vision for the future. Highlight those individuals who have sacrificed in the past and built the foundation for the present. People love it when past employees are remembered fondly for their part; it gives them confidence that their current work will be remembered and honored. A huge part of leadership is helping employees and constituents remember, and then help them remember again, since we are prone to forget.

Ideas Worth Remembering
Following are some ideas you may have used or might consider to remember those folks who help make your business or ministry meaningful.

- Retirements: We don't want to wait until employees retire to acknowledge their value. Retirement celebrations should be a no-holds-barred attempt to honor their years of service and work accomplishments.

- Employee Recognition: This idea has been around for a long time, but it still is appreciated by most employees. We enjoy the recognition for years of service, but service anniversaries also give leaders an opportunity to express their appreciation to a specific employee and share thoughts on how that person has contributed to the company.

- Orientations: Many companies have orientation programs, so why not build into the curriculum the past accomplishments of the company as new employees are added?

- Employee Evaluations: Most employees don't like evaluations, but this can be both a time to encourage them or confront them on their work. Years ago, I designed an evaluation that used the job description as the base line and asked the employee and supervisor to evaluate the employee's performance against the base. This two-sided evaluation is a powerful tool that provides input from the employee and their boss. The often-dreaded evaluation became an opportunity to remember their accomplishments and encourage the employee, as well as set goals for the next evaluation period.

- Leadership Diary: I'm a huge fan of keeping a prayer journal/diary. I came across this idea more than 30 years ago and I can't tell how many times my journal has been a source of remembrance and encouragement. Make short entries in your journal or organizer that help you remember accomplishments and the people who made things happen. Then use that entry in preparing for the next opportunity to bring the employees together to remember.

Reflections on Leadership:

1. Grab your journal and a cup of coffee as you reflect upon the idea of remembering. A leader needs to help those they lead remember what has been accomplished.

   • Journal those milestones that have made your company or ministry what it is today. In reviewing your list, you might see some events that need to be remembered and celebrated.

   • I've talked about the importance of remembering, but you need to think this through and come to your own conclusion. Is remembering an important leadership activity? Why or why not?

2. Mnemonics: People want and need to remember, so what do you currently do at your company or ministry to help people remember accomplishments? What can you do to better remember?

3. Review the following quotes about the importance of remembering and apply.

   • *"So long as the memory of certain beloved friends lives in my heart, I shall say that life is good."* Helen Keller

   • *"Life is all memory, except for the one present moment that goes by you so quickly you hardly catch it going."* Tennessee Williams

#7: JUDGES

Leadership is Job One!

- *The Spirit of the LORD came upon him (Othniel, Caleb's younger brother), so that he became Israel's judge and went to war . . . (3:10)*

- *Once again the Israelites did evil in the eyes of the LORD. (3:12)*

- *After Ehud died, the Israelites once again did evil in the eyes of the LORD . . . (4:1)*

- *(Deborah dies) Again the Israelites did evil in the eyes of the LORD . . . (6:1)*

- *When the angel of the LORD appeared to Gideon, he said, "The LORD is with you, mighty warrior." (6:12)*

- *No sooner had Gideon died than the Israelites again prostituted themselves to the Baals. (8:33a)*

- *Abimelech (Gideon's wicked son) son of Jerub-Baal went to his mother's brother's in Shechem and said to them and to all his mother's clan, "Ask all the citizens of Shechem, 'Which is better for you: to have all seventy of Jerub-Baal's sons rule over you, or just one man?'" . . . He went to his father's home in Ophrah and on one stone murdered his seventy brothers . . . (9:1-2, 5)*

- *Again the Israelites did evil in the eyes of the LORD. (After Jephthah dies) (10:6)*

- *Again the Israelites did evil in the eyes of the LORD, so the LORD delivered them into the hands of the Philistines for forty years (The condition of Israel before Samson) (13:1)*

- *In those days Israel had no king; everyone did as they saw fit. (21:25)*

See a pattern in these verses? God-honoring leaders brought blessings to Israel, whereas evil leaders brought bondage. Yet, this pattern of a godly/ungodly leader is repeated countless times in Scripture. Why are these stories of good and bad leaders in the Bible? I believe it is a powerful reminder of our fallen nature and its impact on every aspect of life, as well as the power that is available to a leader who follows the ways of God. Years ago, Ford Motor Company used a catchy slogan: *Quality is Job One.* So too, leadership is job one in a company, ministry or nation.

Does it seem like good leaders are hard to find these days? This feeling isn't new as evidenced by the book of Judges written several millennia ago. God didn't want Israel to have an "earthly" leader; He wanted them to be a people content with His oversight through a priestly line. Israel shunned theocracy when Samuel's sons led through bribery and perverted justice (I Samuel 8:3) and asked for a king to lead them (I Samuel 8:6).

Godly leadership is summed up in Samuel's farewell comments:

> As for me, I am old and gray, and my sons are here with you. I have been your leader from my youth until this day. Here I stand. Testify against me in the presence of the LORD and his anointed. Whose ox have I taken? Whose donkey have I taken? Whom have I cheated? Whom have I oppressed? From whose hand have I accepted a bribe to make me shut my eyes? If I have done any of these, I will make it right. (1 Samuel 12:2-3)

Taking an ox or donkey in Samuel's day is today's equivalent of adjusting financials statements for a shareholder's report, charging too much for goods or services, or cheating another out of their creative property. A godly leader should view each *deal* and *decision* through the perspective of what Christ would do. WWJD might seem "cutesy," but its intent is to remind us of the high standard of following Christ.

A leader's work is job one for any business, because a leader maintains the mission, crafts a vision and plans to move toward a strategic position. You communicate to various publics and create an effective, harmonic team of other leaders. As a Biblical leader, you must perform at the highest level of competency, but also live a life that mimics Christ in your words, decisions and actions.

Reflections on Leadership:

1. Leadership: Take your journal and consider why leadership is vital to a company, ministry or nation. What conclusions did you discover and how might they impact the way you lead?

    *   What is it about leadership and the nature of mankind that drives some leaders to move toward the dark side of leadership? Are you trending toward the dark side?

    *   Ask your team or direct reports to evaluate their leadership to see if bad leadership is creeping into the ranks. This exercise could be a platform for you, as a Biblical leader, to define the expectations you require for leading in the company you oversee.

2. Reflect on the following quotes about the importance of leadership and journal any implications this exercise might have on your leading.

    *   *"Leadership is a potent combination of strategy and character. But if you must be without one, be without the strategy."* General H. Norman Schwarzkopf

    *   *"Leadership is getting someone to do what they don't want to do in order to achieve what they want to achieve."* Tom Landry

#8: RUTH

A Good Man is Hard to Find

Boaz replied, "I've been told all about what you have done for your mother-in-law since the death of your husband . . . " (2:11)

"He has not stopped showing his kindness to the living and the dead." (2:20)

In the middle of the night something startled the man, and he turned and discovered a woman lying at his feet. (3:8)

"And now, my daughter, don't be afraid. I will do for you all you ask. All my fellow townsmen know that you are a woman of noble character. Although it is true that I am near of kin, there is a kinsman-redeemer nearer than I." (3:10b-12)

So the kinsman-redeemer said to Boaz, "Buy it yourself." And he removed his sandal. Then Boaz announced to the elders and all the people, "Today you are witnesses that I have bought from Naomi all the property of Elimelech, Kilion and Mahlon. I have also acquired Ruth the Moabitess, Mahlon's widow, as my wife, in order to maintain the name of the dead with his property, so that his name will not disappear from among his family or from the town records. Today you are witnesses!" (4:8-10)

A Good Man is Hard to Find is the title of a 1953 short story by Flannery O'Conner—it is also a truism. I sometimes kid my three daughters (two already married) that their mother got the last good man. The two married daughters vehemently disagree, citing their husbands as examples.

It does appear that "good men" are hard to find. We can illustrate this with countless recent examples of men who lack integrity as well as the scoundrels from Scriptures: Judas Iscariot, Pontius Pilate, Pharaoh, Herod and many kings of the Northern and Southern Kingdoms. We love the book of Ruth with its storyline of love, loyalty and redemption through the work of a good man, Boaz.

This leadership story illustrates how Boaz was a good man in the way he complimented Ruth for her loyalty to her mother-in-law, Naomi. He also gave special attention to their physical needs, demonstrated appropriate behavior in a potentially compromising situation and went above and beyond to ensure kinsman-redeemer protocol was followed.

Take the time to read this remarkable book through the eyes of Boaz. Indeed, Ruth is the main character in the story, because of her response to Naomi's guidance, but Boaz's contribution can't be overlooked, especially since Boaz served honorably by taking fiduciary responsibility for Elimelech's family. Some scholars also interpret Boaz's work as a metaphor for our ultimate Redeemer (Isaiah 43:14).

A Biblical leader will exemplify Boaz-like behavior in his life. Do you compliment those who demonstrate care for others as Ruth did for Naomi? Have you shown above reproach behavior with those of the opposite sex in situations where you might have gotten away with it—as Boaz did when Ruth lay at his feet? Do you go above and beyond taking care of the needs of those who work for you as Boaz did by instructing his workers to leave a little more in the field for Ruth? For example, I know a CEO who provides small, no interest loans to employees who find themselves in short-term need. Such a simple idea has engendered tremendous loyalty for this CEO because of his extra care for their personal needs.

Ronald Reagan's humorous statement about character, "You can tell a lot about a fellow's character by the way he eats jelly beans." is a poor way to evaluate character. However, if I followed you for a day, I could tell much about your character through your words (public and private), what you do with your time and money and the way you treat others. Are you a good man or woman seeking to honor God or are you like most leaders, leading without regard for God and His cause?

Reflections on Leadership:

1. Have you demonstrated some of the behavior that Boaz showed in complimenting others, taking care in relationships with the opposite sex, caring for those who work with or for you and sometimes taking the financial burden of others in your family?

2. Why is it important for a person of faith to demonstrate their faith in the way they live? After all, our faith isn't contingent on works, rather on faith in the work of Christ. Look at the following Scriptures to determine your answer: Galatians 6:1-10; Ephesians 2:8-9; Philippians 3:1-21; James 2:14-26.

3. Review the following quotes on character and write your thoughts and their implications in your journal.

    *   *"The people have a right, an indisputable, unalienable, indefeasible, divine right to the most dreaded and envied kind of knowledge—I mean of the character and conduct of their rulers."* John Adams

    *   *"Character cannot be developed in ease and quiet. Only through experience of trial and suffering can the soul be strengthened, vision cleared, ambition inspired and success achieved."* Helen Keller

#9: 1 SAMUEL

Desperate Times Call for Desperate Measures

Saul had expelled the mediums and spiritists from the land. The Philistines assembled and came and set up camp at Shunem, while Saul gathered all the Israelites and set up camp at Gilboa. When Saul saw the Philistine army, he was afraid; terror filled his heart. He inquired of the LORD, but the LORD did not answer him by dreams or Urim or prophets. Saul then said to his attendants, "Find me a woman who is a medium, so I may go and inquire of her."

"There is one in Endor," they said.

So Saul disguised himself, putting on other clothes, and at night he and two men went to the woman. "Consult a spirit for me," he said, "and bring up for me the one I name."

But the woman said to him, "Surely you know what Saul has done. He has cut off the mediums and spiritists from the land. Why have you set a trap for my life to bring about my death?" (28:3b-9)

"Desperate times call for desperate measures" is one of those quotes without a clear history—some believe it was originated by Hippocrates. We don't know its origin, but we know what it means. When we face extreme challenges, we need to use extraordinary action to address them. Most often, this quote is used by those facing desperate times not of their making. However, it could apply to leaders who face desperate times of their own making, as with this leadership story from the Bible.

Our story is about a king who faced a life and death situation and resorted to means that he had outlawed. Saul was the anointed ruler of Israel (1 Samuel 26:11), yet he often acted duplicitously and lost his head with jealousy toward

David, who would become king. Saul showed great leadership stature early in office, but lost his throne because of his impetuousness that led to disobedience (1 Samuel 28:17).

I remember reading the Witch of Endor story for the first time as a teenager. I was fascinated with Saul's fall from a pinnacle of power (an impressive young man without equal among Israelites—a head taller than any of the others. 1 Samuel 9:2b) to desperately seeking the voice of God through a fortune-teller.

How could this happen? In Saul's case it was his impatience and an "above the law" attitude in preparing a burnt offering to inquire of God as to the outcome of a battle with the Philistines (1 Samuel 13:5-14). He thought, "I waited seven days for Samuel and he's not here and I need an answer now." This same mindset was manifested by Saul's seeking out a medium to discover the outcome of a battle (1 Samuel 28:3b-31:5). The enemy, again the Philistines, were now God's instrument of judgment, killing his sons and mortally wounding Saul, who fell on his sword to escape being taken captive.

Know any leaders who started well and finished in failure? Does Bernie Madoff, Jeffery Skilling or Kenneth Lay ring a bell? Bernie Madoff ran his investment company for almost 50 years. Many believed him to be a man of character before realizing they were part of the largest Ponzi scheme in American history; Jeffery Skilling had an MBA from Harvard and was the youngest partner in McKinsey and Company; and Kenneth Lay's father was a Baptist minister and obtained a Ph.D. in economics before his fall. A leader can have the look, the right academic background, a resume that lists magnificent experiences, the right pedigree and yet fail, if they allow character flaws.

Each of the previously mentioned business leaders faced desperate situations of their own making. They also dealt with them through despicable methods that affected tens of thousands who believed in their leadership.

Have you ever watched a leader take a company into desperate situations because of poor leadership decisions or blinding pride? Did that leader then make more poor decisions, out of desperation, to deal with the mess? How can such scenarios occur with leaders who seem to have it all? God's Word reminds us that our heart is desperately wicked (Jeremiah 17:9) We easily can be influenced by our sinful flesh and a world that worships the antithesis of Scriptural teachings.

Reflections on Leadership:

1. Saul couldn't wait for Samuel before offering a burnt offering and justified this action by saying he needed a decision now. Patience in making decisions is an important aspect of leadership. What does Scripture say about patience and decision-making? Do a search of Scripture on the topic of patience and decision making and how they might relate and write your findings in your journal.

2. Jealousy is a destructive mindset for a leader. Why? Have you ever felt jealous of another with whom you worked? Why were you jealous and how did that feeling have an impact on your leadership?

3. Review the following quotes about desperate times and reflect on your leadership when facing challenges.

    •   *"When you reach the end of your rope, tie a knot and hang on."*
        Abraham Lincoln

    •   *"When you get to that point where you don't want to live, and you don't want to die, it's a desperate, horrible place to be. And I just hit my knees. And I had to use 'The Passion of the Christ' to heal my wounds."* Mel Gibson

#10: 2 SAMUEL

Are You Using All at Your Disposal?

Once more the Philistines came up and spread out in the Valley of Rephaim; so David inquired of the LORD, and he answered . . . (5:22, 23)

Then King David went in and sat before the LORD and he said . . . (7:18)

So David prayed . . . (15:31b)

During the reign of David, there was a famine for three successive years; so David sought the face of the LORD. (21:1)

David sang to the LORD the words of this song when the LORD delivered him from the hand of all his enemies and from the hand of Saul. (22:1)

Dr. Tim Irwin, well-known psychologist and author, tells a story about a family vacation that demonstrates the title of this leadership story. His family wanted to take a vacation to Spain, but they needed to keep the cost down. They found a beautiful hotel for a good price. To save money, they brought food with them. However, they noticed how wonderful the food looked at the hotel restaurant, but didn't eat there because of the perceived cost. The irony came at checkout when they were asked if they enjoyed the hotel's accommodations, especially the meals. The Irwin's didn't realize that meals were included in the hotel package! A funny lesson, but sad that the family didn't enjoy the great meals that were at their disposal.

Not taking advantage of free food is one thing, but not taking advantage of all that we have in Christ is quite another. The Scriptures cited from 2 Samuel demonstrate a reason David is called a man after God's heart (Acts 13:22b).

He connected to God through his heart by inquiry, prayer and words of praise. Read the words of David's song from 2 Samuel 22 and you sense a man with a profound understanding of his God. Then, turn in your Bible to Psalms 25 and 32 and read the words of a man who desperately wants God's guidance and forgiveness in his life. After reading such words, you can understand why God calls David a man after His own heart. Not a perfect man, but a man who sought God in his trials and failures.

I often hear Christian leaders express their desire to mature in their faith. At the same time I hear of their struggle balancing the demands of life: faith, family and the marketplace. One of the best ways to ensure our relationship with the Father remains central in our lives, is to look at Christ's life during his earthly ministry. Theologically, we know that Christ was more than mere man and was the unique blending of God and man (what theologians call the Hypostatic Union). He showed His priority of fellowshipping with His Father as seen in the following Scriptures:

> *Very early in the morning, while it was still dark, Jesus got up, left the house and went off to a solitary place, where he prayed.* (Mark 1:35)

> *At daybreak, Jesus went out to a solitary place.* (Luke 4:42)

I'm sure you have read these Scriptures, yet, have you mused upon what they mean for your faith walk? If Christ (remember He was a God/man) required time alone with His Father to process His life, how much more do we need time alone with the Father to process all that life throws at us? We need to seriously grapple with this rhetorical question since many of us struggle with keeping the faith component of life as our priority.

Time alone with God is an imperative. It lays the foundation for the day to be built upon. We cannot spend time in prayer, seeking the mind of God, without coming away with a better understanding of who He is and what we are. Yet, prayer is often the thing we scratch from our calendar when the pace of the day quickens. Ironic, isn't it? We sometimes eliminate the one thing from our life that prepares us best for the challenges and opportunities of the day.

Consider the following quotes about the value of time with God. Note that those quoted are people that God used greatly for His cause. A correlation?

> Pray often; for prayer is a shield to the soul, a sacrifice to God, and a scourge for Satan. —John Bunyan

> To be a Christian without prayer is no more possible than to be alive without breathing. —Martin Luther King, Jr.

Are you using all that is at your disposal as a leader? You probably start the day with strong coffee and a trade publication. There is nothing wrong with strong coffee (my beverage of choice) or reading material germane to your profession, but today we live in a nanosecond world which demands even greater attention to "being still" before our God. Dallas Willard, college professor and spiritual author often said, "You must ruthlessly eliminate hurry from your life." Time with the Father, far and away, gives you the perspective that few have. Inquire, pray and sing praise to the Father. Abide in Him (John 15:1-17) and you will tap into the greatest power in the Universe that allows you to use everything at your disposal.

Reflections on Leadership:

1. An experiment: Set aside three days next week in which you will commit to rise at least 30 minutes earlier than normal to read the Bible and pray. For some of you this isn't an experiment, but your regular routine; but for others this will be a challenge. I'd like you to write a short entry in your journal about how the days went that began with God versus those that didn't. Did you sense or see any differences? What conclusions can you draw from this experiment?

2. Write the following Bible passages out in your journal and memorize those Scriptures that speak to this idea of time with God: 2 Chronicles 7:14, Psalm 5:3; 37:7; 50:15; 145:18; Luke 11:1-13; 18:1-10; 1 Corinthians 14:15; Philippians 4:6, Colossians 4:2; 1 Timothy 2:1-4; James 1:7, 4:3, 5:13-16; 1 John 5:14-15

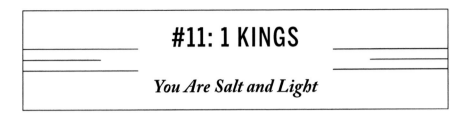

#11: 1 KINGS

You Are Salt and Light

Now the famine was severe in Samaria and Ahab had summoned Obadiah, who was in charge of the palace (Obadiah was a devout believer in the LORD. While Jezebel was killing off the LORD's prophets, Obadiah had taken a hundred prophets and hidden them in two caves, fifty in each and had supplied them with food and water.) (18:2b-4)

This leadership story is for those who work in the marketplace and report to a difficult person or work in a challenging environment. Can any of you relate?

Obadiah had a significant leadership position overseeing King Ahab's palace. If you don't know what kind of leader Ahab was, read 1 Kings 18-22. His reign is summed up in 1 Kings 21:25a: *There was never a man like Ahab, who sold himself to do evil in the eyes of the LORD, urged on by Jezebel his wife. He behaved in the vilest manner by going after idols.* You think you report to a difficult person: Obadiah, all the more.

Many Christian leaders find themselves in godless business settings. This world is an evil place, as we are reminded by Paul in Ephesians 2:1-3.

As for you, you were dead in your transgressions and sins, in which you used to live when you followed the ways of this world and of the ruler of the kingdom of the air, the spirit who is now at work in those who are disobedient. All of us also lived among them at one time, gratifying the cravings of our sinful nature and following its desires and thoughts. Like the rest, we were by nature objects of wrath. (Ephesians 2:1-3)

The earth is influenced by Satan and his minions, so the business world will not be like church. Business can be a contrary place for Christian leaders who find themselves in scenarios that challenge the way you talk and make decisions and stretch you away from your faith. Yet, it is in this environment that you can best shine as light and season like salt.

As an Obadiah in the marketplace, you might even be misunderstood by other people of faith. They may wrongly lump you in with all the negative they hear about the business world while making you feel "sub-Christian" for being part of that evil business. Frankly, we need more Obadiah's who will work where evil dwells and serve as an influence for good. Evil grows when left unchecked by good.

Paul, found himself in a godless environment during his prison stay before seeing the emperor. In his letter to the Philippians, he writes about the opportunity he had:

> *Now I want you to know, brothers, that what has happened to me has really served to advance the gospel. As a result, it has become clear throughout the whole palace guard and to everyone else that I am in chains for Christ. Because of my chains, most of the brothers in the Lord have been encouraged to speak the word of God more courageously and fearlessly.* (Philippians 1:12-14)

When we read this passage, it should remind us that our lives are superintended by God to position us for the greatest influence. Yes, even if it means that we are selected to be the queen of an evil empire or to go to prison for no good reason other than our faith.

If you haven't noticed, the world is not populated by a majority of Christians. However, we are called to be an influence for righteousness, so as you live your life in this evil world, you are to be God's living letters (2 Corinthians 3:2, 3), because most folks aren't going to Christian bookstores to buy a Bible. Are you in politics? Be a letter of Christ like my friend, Trent Franks, who is a U. S. Congressman from Arizona. Are you in movies? Be a letter of Christ like John Schneider, who came to faith in Christ through Johnny Cash and wants to use his platform in Hollywood for good. Are you a CEO? Be a living letter like R. G. LeTourneau, who lived on 10 percent of his income, started a Christian college and became one of the greatest inventors and business leaders of our times, as well as an influence for God in the marketplace.

Be an Obadiah in the king's palace, making a difference in a place that desperately needs your witness. God may well have placed you in the middle of the battle for the hearts and minds of those you work with. Be strong, be brave, be courageous and may you see the power of God in your life and your impact in the marketplace.

Reflections on Leadership:

1. Marketplace environment: Are you, like Obadiah, in an environment that is unfriendly to your faith?

   • Have you felt a sense of calling to this situation to serve as a witness?

   • Have you considered leaving because the pressure is too much to bear?

2. Journal: Write the names of those co-workers whom you would like to engage in a spiritual discussion. Think about how you might open the door to talk about your faith. Take your journal and write your thoughts on how these faith interactions went.

3. Read the following quotes and consider how living your faith where you are is critical.

   • *"Do all the good you can. By all the means you can. In all the ways you can. In all the places you can. At all the times you can. To all the people you can. As long as ever you can."* John Wesley

   • *"I'm a dreamer and continue to dream of what can and will be, Expecting great things from God, Attempting great things for God."* William Carey, Father of Modern Missions

#12: 2 KINGS

Epitaph

Furthermore, Josiah got rid of the mediums and spiritists, the household gods, the idols and all the other detestable things seen in Judah and Jerusalem. This he did to fulfill the requirements of the law written in the book that Hilkiah the priest had discovered in the temple of the LORD. Neither before nor after Josiah was there a king like him who turned to the LORD as he did—with all his heart and with all his soul and with all his strength, in accordance with all the Law of Moses. (23:24-25)

Thomas Jefferson's epitaph reads:

Author of the Declaration of American Independence, of the Statute of Virginia for Religious Freedom, and the Father of the University of Virginia

Jefferson lived a remarkable life, as depicted by his epitaph. Few have influenced what America became more than Jefferson. Much conjecture surrounds Jefferson's faith, but we know exactly where King Josiah stood with God.

2 Kings 22:25 is a remarkable epitaph about King Josiah's leadership, an example for all leaders. At the ripe age of 26, he sent his secretary and skilled artisans to rebuild the temple. Through this refurbishment process, they discovered the Book of the Law (2 Kings 22:8), a book that contained teachings that were foreign to the nation of Judah. Josiah demonstrated great leadership in recognizing the value of the Book of the Law. He rightly humbled himself before God (2 Kings 22:11) and realized that his nation had neglected God's teachings and was worthy of judgment. His humility saved Judah from judgment (2 Kings 22:19, 20), and he went on to reactivate a covenant with God.

Then the king called together all the elders of Judah and Jerusalem. He went up to the temple of the LORD with the men of Judah, the people of Jerusalem, the priest and the prophets—all the people from the least to the greatest. He read in their hearing all the words of the Book of the Covenant, which had been found in the temple of the LORD. The king stood by the pillar and renewed the covenant in the presence of the LORD—to follow the LORD and keep his commands, regulations and decrees with all his heart and all his soul, thus confirming the words of the covenant written in this book. Then, all the people pledged themselves to the covenant. (2 Kings 23:1-3)

Leadership! What a powerful force in a country, a ministry and a business. However, leadership can have a dark side. Hitler said, "What luck for rulers that men do not think." We know the rest of this story from history, how Hitler's statement rang true with an entire country.

Where Hitler provides an ultimate example of leadership evil, Josiah provides the polar opposite through leading his nation into radical change and commitment. Leadership has the potential for great evil as well as great good. As a leader whose life has been changed through your faith in Christ, you have a responsibility to use your leadership position for the cause of Christ and to lead from a Biblical mindset.

What will your epitaph say about your role as a leader? Will it talk about your hubris, greed or unethical business tactics? May it never be said of a Christian leader that they led from such platforms. Rather, may our tombstones state the godly character traits that were demonstrated in our leadership.

Josiah demonstrated remarkable leadership for a young king. His leadership changed the lives of an entire nation. Think about the difference you make, or can make, in countless lives in the company or ministry you oversee! Leadership is a gifting of the Spirit (Romans 12:8b), even though there are great leaders who have no faith. Faith adds a dimension to leadership that relates to the value of people. There is nothing in this world of greater value than people. Since it is obvious that employees are people, a Christian leader must have their well-being in the forefront of his or her thinking. Sometimes this priority for people rubs the business world the wrong way when decisions are driven only by the "bottom line".

King Josiah left a great leadership legacy for us to learn from today. What can we learn and apply to our leadership from this king who totally turned to his God? How can we be God's instrument in the lives of those we lead through our decisions and leadership?

Reflections on Leadership:

1. Is there a situation where your management team or employees need to make a commitment to a mission or vision that will better the product or services from your business? How might you help your employees make this commitment, and how does the story of Josiah's leadership to commitment help you think this through?

2. Epitaph: You just learned that you have weeks to live. What would your epitaph say about your life's balance, your leadership and your relationships? You just learned you have 30 more years to lead. How would your leadership change, and what would your ideal epitaph say?

3. Reflect on the following quotes about a person's epitaph.

    *   *"Live so that when the final summons comes you will leave something more behind you than an epitaph on a tombstone or an obituary in a newspaper."* Billy Sunday, evangelist and professional baseball player

    *   *"I haven't written my own epitaph, and I'm not sure I should. Whatever it is, I hope it will be simple, and that it will point people not to me, but to the One I served."* Billy Graham

#13: 1 CHRONICLES

They Aim to Please

David was staying in the stronghold at the time, and a Philistine detachment had occupied the town of Bethlehem. David remarked longingly to his men, "Oh, how I would love some of that good water from the well by the gate in Bethlehem." So the three broke through the Philistine lines, drew some water from the well by the gate in Bethlehem, and brought it back to David. But David refused to drink it. Instead, he poured it out as an offering to the LORD. "God forbid that I should drink this!" he exclaimed. "This water is as precious as the blood of these men who risked their lives to bring it to me." So David did not drink it. (11:16-19) NLT

This passage tells us of David's first encounter with the Philistines, about five miles from Bethlehem. With the Philistine army located between David and the well, fetching him a drink of water was incredibly risky for his men.

Three of David's mighty men apparently had no problem risking their lives to fulfill a frivolous wish by their leader. Then, what did these mighty men think when David poured the water on the ground—water they risked their lives for?

The text tells us that David poured the water out as a sacrifice, so we don't need to speculate about his reason for doing something so unexpected. How was pouring the water on the ground a sacrifice? As I reread the text and several commentaries, the meaning became clear. David realized that his request for water put his mighty men in harm's way. So, rather than quench his thirst, he offered it as a sacrifice to God. His pouring the water on the ground was the right thing to do when he realized his faux pas. I'm sure the mighty men were initially shocked by their king's action, but later understood that their commander realized the folly of his request.

Leaders must realize that those who report to them aim to please. This point was demonstrated to me as a young vice president at a well-known Christian college. The president told me that while walking down a hallway that had just been painted a shade of beige, he made a statement about how nice the walls looked. He also mentioned in passing that his favorite color was blue. The next day he passed through the same hallway and was surprised to see it was now blue! Without being asked to change the color, the painters repainted the walls the president's favorite color with an aim to please. Repainting a wall isn't as dangerous as fetching water near the enemy camp but both groups just wanted to please their leader.

It's great that people want to please their leaders, and leaders need to realize the power of their words. The book of James contains a challenging passage about the importance of our words. These verses are directed at teachers of God's Word, but applicable to all leaders as well.

> *Not many of you should presume to be teachers, my brothers, because you know that we who teach will be judged more strictly. We all stumble in many ways. <u>If anyone is never at fault in what he says, he is a perfect man, able to keep his whole body in check</u>.* (James 3:1, 2)

Our words are the litmus test of our faith. If we use them with propriety, we are perfect. Well, how are you doing with this exam of your faith? How many times have I opened my mouth and inserted my foot? A leader's words are their greatest asset. They can encourage or crush, motivate or stifle, give direction or express ambiguity. Words can also express a person's character by making selfish or inappropriate requests of those who work for them. Watch the news this week and see how many leaders misuse their position by asking others to do something that is wrong.

A Christian leader must be sensitive to the power of words and how they reflect your relationship with the Savior. Sometimes, the best way to show this sensitivity is to use fewer words, as is stated in the following verse.

My dear brothers, take note of this: Everyone should be quick to listen, slow to speak and slow to become angry. (James 1:19)

David's desire for a drink might be fine under different circumstances, but when his words endangered his men, he was completely out of line. He did the right thing in pouring the water out as an offering. Do you admit it when you say something inappropriate or frivolous? Better to admit you said the wrong thing than dig in your heels and let pride and shame rule your next words.

Reflections on Leadership:

1. One of the most powerful passages in the Bible on the power of words is in James 3:1-12. Take your journal and write this passage out and then read it several times. What did you learn from reading this passage about words and how they can be a great force for good and evil? Consider how your words are one of the most important aspects of your leadership and make a journal entry concerning your desire to use your words more carefully.

2. Review this story with your direct reports and discuss the power of words. Talk with the team about holding one another accountable for the words they use. Consider how this exercise could impact your business in motivating employees and setting a tone of character in the marketplace through the appropriate use of words.

3. Following are a couple quotes about the power of words. Please reflect and apply.

    *   *"You have it easily in your power to increase the sum total of this world's happiness now. How? By giving a few words of sincere appreciation to someone who is lonely or discouraged. Perhaps you will forget tomorrow the kind words you say today, but the recipient may cherish them over a lifetime."* Dale Carnegie

    *   *"Words are, of course, the most powerful drug used by mankind."* Rudyard Kipling

#14: 2 CHRONICLES

Formulas for Success

If my people, who are called by my name, will humble themselves and pray and seek my face and turn from their wicked ways, then will I hear from heaven and will forgive their sin and will heal their land. Now my eyes will be open and my ears attentive to the prayers offered in this place. I have chosen and consecrated this temple so that my Name may be there forever. My eyes and my heart will always be there.

As for you, if you walk before me faithfully as David your father did, and do all I command, and observe my decrees and laws, I will establish your royal throne, as I covenanted with David your father when I said, 'You shall never fail to have a man to rule over Israel.'

But, if you turn away and forsake the decrees and commands I have given you and go off to serve other gods and worship them, then I will uproot Israel from my land, which I have given them, and will reject this temple I have consecrated for my Name. (7:14-20a)

When I started my teaching career, almost 40 years ago, I taught high school science. One course that challenged me was chemistry. Although I struggled to keep one-step ahead of the students, I appreciated this subject because it used formulas. In chemistry, a formula is a set of chemical symbols showing the elements present in a compound and their relative proportions. Simply put, a formula shows how chemicals react to one another and the outcome of this reaction. In essence, the cited Scripture below provides three formulas to gain God's blessing.

This passage from 2 Chronicles 7 follows King Solomon's dedication of the permanent temple that would hold the furnishings to enable the priests to perform their duties. The Lord appears to Solomon at night (much like He appeared to Solomon in 2 Chronicles 1:7 when he asked for wisdom and knowledge to lead the people) following his dedication and gives formulas for Solomon and Israel to follow that would ensure God's blessing. These formulas are:

1. If the people humble themselves, seek Him, change their ways and ask forgiveness = God will hear, heal their land and forgive their sins.

2. If Solomon obeys the law, as his father did = God will establish his throne.

3. If Solomon serves other gods = God will uproot Israel from the land.

Pretty simple, huh? Indeed, these formulas are simple, but apparently difficult to grasp since the remainder of this book lists kings who failed to honor and obey God. Even Solomon drifted from his moorings of honoring God. He initiated a drift that would divide his country.

The old hymn states the truths of these formulas with such clarity: "Trust and obey, for there's no other way to be happy in Jesus, but to trust and obey." Obedience is something we often talk about in the church; however, actually obeying is quite another thing. The three formulas in this leadership story converge into one idea: obeying God's Law (His Word). If a leader or a nation deviates from obeying God's laws, there will be ramifications. At the point that a leader or nation realizes their disobedience, they must confess, repent (change direction) and seek His mercy.

Israel had the promise of land for an inheritance, and Solomon that his throne would continue on; but we know the rest of the story, that they failed to keep their end of the deal. As we read Scripture, we see that leaders have a key role in helping stay the course. Pastors as they lead the church, CEOs as they lead businesses and leaders as they direct nations are called to lead in accordance with the tenets of God's Word. Obey, obey, obey should be a leader's mantra as they take the mantle of leadership. A.W. Tozer (author of over 40 books such as *The Pursuit of God* and *The Knowledge of the Holy*) states this in the following quote:

The man that believes will obey; failure to obey is convincing proof that there is no true faith present. To attempt the impossible God must give faith or there will be none, and He gives faith to the obedient heart only.

Reflections on Leadership:

1. What do you think of this idea that a formula outlines how a leader or nation receives the blessings of God?

2. How does this leadership lesson align with what is happening in America? We must be careful in equating America with God's "Chosen People," Israel, but the principle of a nation turning back to God and His mercy are a truism. Therefore, as a leader, how can your leadership or company help turn this country back from disobedience?

3. Reflect on the following quotes in your journal:

   • *"He has the right to interrupt your life. He is Lord. When you accepted Him as Lord, you gave Him the right to help Himself to your life anytime He wants."* Henry Blackaby, pastor and author of *Experiencing God*

   • *"[The natural man] knows that if the spiritual life gets hold of it, all its self-centeredness and self-will are going to be killed and it is ready to fight tooth and nail to avoid that."* C.S. Lewis

#15: EZRA

Leadership Multiplication

After these things, during the reign of Artaxerxes king of Persia, Ezra son of Seraiah, the son of Azariah, the son of Hilkiah, the son of Shallum, the son of Zadok, the son of Ahitub, the son of Amariah, the son of Azariah, the son of Meraioth, the son of Zerahiah, the son of Uzzi, the son of Bukki, the son of Abishua, the son of Phinehas, the son of Eleazar, the son of Aaron the chief priest—this Ezra came up from Babylon. He was a teacher well versed in the Law of Moses, which the LORD, the God of Israel, had given. The king had granted him everything he asked, for the hand of the LORD God was on him. (7:1-6)

For Ezra had devoted himself to the study and observance of the Law of the LORD, and to teaching its decrees and laws in Israel. (7:10)

And you, Ezra, in accordance with the wisdom of your God, which you possess, appoint magistrates and judges to administer justice to all the people of Trans-Euphrates—all who know the laws of your God. And you are to teach any who do not know them. (7:25)

That's a lot of strange-sounding names before we hear about Ezra! I hope you noticed that Ezra is from the lineage of the first priest, Aaron. Pretty impressive pedigree and it shows in his leadership in this most challenging situation.

Some background is needed to understand what Ezra faced. You might remember that there were three periods of deportation to Babylon (605, 597 and 586 B.C.) and three periods of returning from exile (538, 458 and 444 B.C.). The book of Ezra covers two periods when some of the exiled Jews returned to Jerusalem and outlines the work that needed to be done before the wall could be rebuilt. Chapters 1-6 of Ezra tell about the rebuilding of the temple (also described in the books of Haggai and Zechariah), and chapters

7-10 describe a reformation that Ezra led, since the Jews had disobeyed God through intermarriage with other nations. Today, we don't think anything of marrying someone from another country, but remember Israel was called to a special purpose in God's plan of redemption. The third period of returning from exile is explained in the book of Nehemiah, when the Jerusalem wall was completed under Nehemiah's leadership.

I selected this passage because it tells us about the special work Ezra did in teaching the Law of Moses (Ezra 7:25): replicating what he knew and creating spiritual leaders. His teaching was mission critical since it helped the people understand their sin through knowledge of the Law, and then crafted an action plan to deal with their sin and helped prepare the nation for the third wave of Jews returning to rebuild the wall.

Ezra replicated himself through his teaching and laid a foundation for Israel's future. With teaching and training in mind, it seems to me that a leader has two primary responsibilities—there are many others—but I feel these two are things that leaders can't delegate. The first is to cast a vision of what the organization is to become, and the second is replicating themselves through the selection, training and supervision of other leaders.

Keeping the two primary leadership tasks in mind, have you ever worked with a leader who thinks they have to do it all, or that no one else can do it like they can? I suspect such a leader doesn't see the importance of training since they aren't interested in developing other leaders or sharing their leadership.

Such leaders are:

- Frustrated, because they think others aren't pulling their weight when in fact the leader isn't permitting them. Good people will leave under this leadership style.

- Ineffective, because they can only do so much and miss the benefit of replicating themselves through other competent leaders who share the leadership load and expand the leader's influence.

- Imbalanced, since they are doing it all and not accomplishing what they desire, they work even harder yet are unable to find balance in life.

As Christian leaders we certainly buy into the importance of training in our company or ministry. However, we understand that training has its limitations if its foundation is solely based on human insight. Have you considered how you might use your position to influence the philosophy and curriculum your company uses by adding the dimension of faith? I am not suggesting that you turn company training into a Bible Study, but you might be able to influence training in subtle, yet profound ways.

Reflections on Leadership:

1. I asked you earlier if you ever worked for a leader who did everything themselves. Now, I'd like to ask if *you* might be that leader. Do you do too much and stymie the growth of others? Do you frustrate others on your team because they can't please you because their work just isn't good enough? Have you lost balance in your life because you are doing more than you should and hinder the replication that could take place with other leaders on your team? Answer these questions in your journal and discuss your answers with your direct reports. What did they say about your answers?

2. Use your journal to reflect on the following quotes.

    *   *"Leadership and learning are indispensable to each other."* John F. Kennedy

    *   *"We now accept the fact that learning is a lifelong process of keeping abreast of change. And the most pressing task is to teach people how to learn."* Peter Drucker

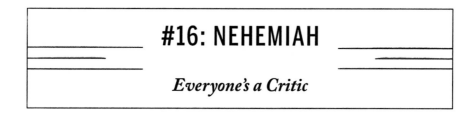

#16: NEHEMIAH

Everyone's a Critic

When Sanballat the Horonite and Tobiah the Ammonite official heard about this, they were very much disturbed that someone had come to promote the welfare of the Israelites. (2:10)

They replied, "Let us start rebuilding." So they began this good work. But when Sanballat the Horonite, Tobiah the Ammonite official and Geshem the Arab heard about it, they mocked and ridiculed us. (2:18b19a)

When Sanballat heard that we were rebuilding the wall, he became angry and greatly incensed. He ridiculed the Jews, and in the presence of his associates and the army of Samaria, he said, "What are those feeble Jews doing? Will they restore their wall? Will they offer sacrifices? Will they finish in a day? Can they bring the stones back to life from those heaps of rubble—burned as they are?" Tobiah the Ammonite, who was at his side, said, "What they are building—if even a fox climbed up on it, he would break down their wall of stones!" (4:1-3)

As a leader, you hear comments like those of Sanballat and Tobiah all the time. They come from your critics, the skeptics, those who know better than you and who will remind you when your idea fails to produce. Welcome to the world of leadership. It is NOT for the faint at heart, as the following quote by Theodore Roosevelt demonstrates:

> It is not the critic who counts; not the man who points out how the strong man stumbles, or where the doer of deeds could have done them better. The credit belongs to the man who is actually in the arena, whose face is marred by dust and sweat and blood, who strives valiantly; errs, who and comes short again and again, because there

is no effort without error and shortcomings; but who does actually strive to do the deeds; who knows the great enthusiasm, the great devotion, who spends himself in a worthy cause; who at the best knows in the end the triumph of high achievement, and who at the worst, if he fails, at least he fails while daring greatly, so that his place shall never be with those cold and timid souls who neither know victory nor defeat.

You know the story from the book of Nehemiah, the story of a cupbearer to the most powerful man alive in his time, who was so moved by the need to rebuild the walls of Jerusalem that he asked his boss for a leave of absence and the resources to do the impossible. The book of Nehemiah is a book about and for leaders! It is replete with leadership principles taken from every possible scenario a leader will face during their career. Our leadership story this time is about the detractors, the critics, the naysayers, the "I told you so" people, the second guessers—anyone who wants to see you fail. They are the thorns in your side, the ones that you hate to have around you.

Critics will always be there, so maybe understanding their role in your life might make their presence tolerable. Have you ever considered how critics might make you a better leader? Their comments could drive you the extra mile with your due diligence, they might make you slow down the decision-making process or they might even help you see the other side of an issue where you might have a blind spot. So, do critics have value? I'm sure you are saying I'm crazy at this point, but viewing criticism this way might help you through that next confrontation with the critics in your life.

Nehemiah's critics didn't think much of his plan because they didn't understand how much rebuilding Jerusalem's wall meant to the Israelites. Today, many critics view Christian leaders as alien because their worldview is at odds with theirs, and perceive ours as foolishness (1 Corinthians 1:18-31).

Christian leaders sometimes have a difficult time with critics. They are taught in Scripture to respect those in authority, so they believe that respect should automatically be shown toward their leadership. Of course, this is a naïve view, given the reality of leading in a fallen world. People, whether believers or unbelievers, struggle with leadership because people simply don't like being led.

The next time critics raise their ugly voices, understand that human beings are critical by nature, so they will be an ever-present part of your world. Then, view criticism as something that could make your leadership better from either hearing the truth in the criticism or making you more careful in your decisions, knowing critics are always watching.

Reflections on Leadership:

1. Think back over your leadership career and identify those who criticized your leadership. Was there any truth in their comments or anything that you learned from their criticisms? Write your thoughts in your journal.

2. Read and write the following Scriptures in your journal and reflect on these verses for coping with critics: Proverbs 26:4; Matthew 7:1-5; 2 Timothy 2:24-25; 4:14-18; James 1:19-20; 2 Peter 3:3-4.

3. Consider the following quotes about critics and write your thoughts in your journal:

   • *"Criticism may not be agreeable, but it is necessary. It fulfills the same function as pain in the human body. It calls attention to an unhealthy state of things."* Winston Churchill

   • *"Don't let an arrow of criticism pierce your heart unless it passes through the filter of Scripture."* Erwin McManus, pastor

#17: ESTHER

Poetic Justice

During the time Mordecai was sitting at the king's gate, Bigthana and Teresh, two of the king's officers who guarded the doorway, became angry and conspired to assassinate King Xerxes. But Mordecai found out about the plot and told Queen Esther, who in turn reported it to the king, giving credit to Mordecai. (2:21-22)

After these events, King Xerxes honored Haman son of Hammedatha . . . (3:1a)

But Mordecai would not kneel down or pay him honor. (3:2b)

Instead Haman looked for a way to destroy all Mordecai's people, the Jews, throughout the whole kingdom of Xerxes. (3:6b)

So the king took his signet ring from his finger and gave it to Haman son of Hammedatha, the Agagite, the enemy of the Jews. "Keep the money," the king said to Haman," and do with the people as you please." (3:10-11)

His wife Zeresh and all his friends said to him, "Have a gallows built, seventy-five feet high, and ask the king in the morning to have Mordecai handed on it." (5:14a)

When Haman entered, the king asked him, "What should be done for the man the king delights to honor?" . . . "Go at once," the king commanded Haman. "Get the robe and the horse and do just as you have suggested for Mordecai the Jew, who sits at the king's gate." (6:6, 10a)

The king said, "Hang him on it!" So they hanged Haman on the gallows he had prepared for Mordecai. Then the king's fury subsided. (7:9b-10)

I know, this leadership story isn't about Esther, even though it's taken from the Biblical text named after this remarkable woman. But I couldn't resist the "poetic justice" found in the story of Haman and Mordecai.

The phrase 'poetic justice' was first used by British critic Thomas Rymer (c. 1641-1713) in a piece called, *The Tragedies of the Last Age Consider'd*. Rymer wrote about the importance of literature expressing justice through its storyline. Poetic justice is used today as a literary device in which virtue is ultimately rewarded and vice punished.

Dante's *Divine Comedy* is a powerful illustration of poetic justice. In this poem's section *Inferno*, Dante uses the literary device of poetic justice to describe how various sins are judged. For example, those who engaged in the sin of fortune-telling exist in a state with their heads posted backward, thus taking away their ability to see the future.

Esther's storyline about her relative Mordecai and King Xerxes' top man, Haman, is the personification of poetic justice. The story of these two begins with Mordecai overhearing and exposing a plot against the king, yet, he is not recognized for his service to the regime. Later, Haman is angered by Mordecai's insubordination and requests to have the Jews eradicated (remember, Esther is a closet Jewess), which is granted by King Xerxes.

So far, this story is about a man who didn't receive his dues and a man who hates a race of people because of one man. The plot thickens when Haman's wife suggests he build a gallows to hang his enemy. The king, at this point, realizes the great disservice he had done in not recognizing Mordecai's loyalty, so the king asks Haman what he should do for a man who deserves the highest honor in his kingdom (ironic, isn't it?). Prideful Haman tells the king what he would want, thinking it was he who would be honored. Haman's vision of honor was given to Mordecai, and the gallows meant for another was used to hang wicked Haman.

Although this story was written in the 5th century B.C., it is being lived out somewhere in the world today. Countries led by hubris-filled despots attack those who oppose their leadership. Leaders in the corporate world who use their position to destroy another's reputation because they didn't show them the respect they felt they deserved, or their pride drives them to make short-sighted decisions. History will continue to repeat the scenario of evil leadership because mankind's nature is prideful and uses the platform of power whenever it can.

No doubt you have witnessed leaders who use their position and power for evil. You may have even lived through a "Haman" leader who sought to destroy you. It is very possible that you have done something that deserved recognition, but you never got it. These leadership scenarios are common and therefore it's possible that some reading this leadership story harbor ill will because they didn't receive the recognition they felt they deserved, or they work for those who are "out to get them."

The recognition you seek may come—the evil leader may get their "just dessert"—but what if these things don't happen? You can't live life hoping all injustices will be dealt with. Several times in this book we have sought to remind you that this world isn't perfect (Ephesians 2:1-3). As a Christian leader, you understand that God is the judge, and ultimate justice will be served, so rest in this fact and don't fret when you don't get the recognition or the bad guy doesn't get caught.

I'd like you to consider one last thought on the concept of poetic justice—the good guy and bad guy get what they deserve. Take the idea of poetic justice and apply it to Christ and the Cross. The good guy didn't get what He deserved. In fact, Christ was the last person on earth who deserved to suffer for sin. The bad guy (all mankind) got what they didn't deserve, because Christ took our judgment upon Himself. I don't know about you, but I'm thrilled that poetic justice didn't live itself out in my case!

Reflections on Leadership:

1. Bad co-worker: Haman was a scoundrel. Have you ever worked with someone who did everything they could to undermine you? What was the outcome of this situation? Was there poetic justice, or is it unresolved in your mind? Journal your thoughts on this reflection.

2. Review the following quotes about poetic justice and apply to your leadership.

    - *"My argument against God was that the universe seemed so cruel and unjust. But how had I got this idea of just and unjust? A man does not call a line crooked unless he has some idea of a straight line. What was I comparing this universe with when I called it unjust?"* C.S. Lewis, *Mere Christianity*

    - *"As my sufferings mounted I soon realized that there were two ways in which I could respond to my situation -- either to react with bitterness or seek to transform the suffering into a creative force. I decided to follow the latter course."* Martin Luther King Jr.

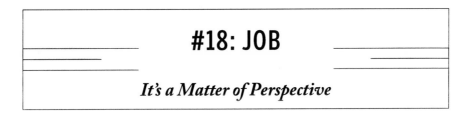

#18: JOB

It's a Matter of Perspective

God's perspective:

> Have you considered my servant, Job? There is no one on earth like him; he is blameless and upright, a man who fears God and shuns evil. (1:8)

> After the LORD had said these things to Job, he said to Eliphaz the Temanite, "I am angry with you and your two friends, because you have not spoken of me what is right, as my servant Job has. (42:7)

Satan's perspective:

> "Skin for skin!" Satan replied. "A man will give all he has for his own life. But now stretch out your hand and strike his flesh and bones, and he will surely curse you to your face." (2:4)

Job's wife's perspective:

> His wife said to him, "Are you still holding on to your integrity? Curse God and die!" (2:9)

Eliphaz's perspective:

> "Is it for your piety that he rebukes you and brings charges against you? Is not your wickedness great?" (22:4, 5a)

Bildad's perspective:

> . . . how much less man, who is but a maggot—a son of man who is only a worm! (25:6)

Elihu's perspective:

> Job says, "I am innocent, but God denies me justice. Although I am right, I am considered a liar; although I am guiltless, his arrow inflicts an incurable wound." (34:5, 6)

Job's perspective:

> *"Naked I came from my mother's womb, and naked I will depart. The LORD gave and the LORD has taken away; may the name of the LORD be praised."* (1:21, 22)

> *"I know that you can do all things; no plan of yours can be thwarted. You asked, 'Who is this that obscures my counsel without knowledge?' Surely I spoke of things I did not understand, things too wonderful for me to know."* (42:2, 3)

I had never read Job from differing perspectives before, but it really helped me understand one of the main themes of this book—everyone thinks their perspective is the right one.

Job was a businessman with considerable wealth and influence, so his calamity brought many out of the woodwork to share their perspective as to why God was judging him.

God viewed Job as a special man. Satan believed Job was like all others and would curse God if turmoil touched his life. Job's wife was tired of the circumstances they faced and just wanted her husband to curse God to end the nightmare. Job's friends believed what most believed, that judgment is the product of one's sin. Finally, Job was trying to understand why God would allow him to go through such devastation, as he had lived an upright life.

Perspective is defined as a particular attitude toward, or way of, regarding something, a point of view. The book of Job certainly fits this definition as has been demonstrated in the previous paragraph. I'd like to take this theme of perspective and apply it to leaders, since it is a challenge to keep one's perspective in a leadership position.

Leadership gives you a certain "perspective" that most don't enjoy. However, this perspective from the corner office can have positive and negative aspects:

- Positive: You should be able to make "better" decisions because you see and know things that help you have additional insight into a situation.

- Negative: Others will often misunderstand or disagree with your decision since they don't have the same perspective.

- Positive: Since you have additional information, you can communicate this perspective to those who will be impacted by your decision and therefore, hopefully help them understand your decision.

- Negative: Just because you have better information shouldn't cause you to ignore or discount input from others. Information doesn't guarantee you will make the right decision, for decisions aren't just about facts. They have to be made in context.

This topic of perspective reminds me of a major faux pas I made 30 years ago when I started my career in higher education. I was working as a dean at a college in Texas at the time. It was the start of the fall semester, and I was giving a student leader a hard time for coming late to a leadership orientation. From my perspective, the student had demonstrated poor leadership by sloughing off his responsibility by coming several days late; however, my perspective was shattered when the young man told me that he was late because his mom had just died! All I cared about was him showing up on campus at the right time, and all he cared about was coping with the devastation that was in his life. Who had the right perspective?

As leaders with faith, we have a spiritual perspective toward life and leadership. This added dimension is misunderstood by the world, but it can provide insight that can enhance our leadership. We can no longer look at our role through the limited vantage point of self, for we are reminded that Biblical leaders should serve and keep pride in check (Philippians 2:7, 8). Another perspective we should never forget is that our plans are only that—our plans. God is God, and we should pray for His insight and blessing in all that we consider doing (James 4:12-17).

Reflections on Leadership:

1. What might you do in your leadership to ensure that you keep the proper perspective of being a servant and a balanced view of pride? Discuss this idea with your direct reports, and ask them to help you keep this perspective in your leadership and the team.

2. Review the following quotes on perspective and write your thoughts in your journal.

   - *"Just because a man lacks the use of his eyes doesn't mean he lacks vision."* Stevie Wonder

   - *"It isn't that they can't see the solution. It is that they can't see the problem."* G.K. Chesterton

#19: PSALMS

Don't Let It Go to Your Head

Do not be overawed when a man grows rich,

when the splendor of his house increases;

for he will take nothing with him when he dies,

his splendor will not descend with him.

Though while he lived he counted himself blessed—

and men praise you when you prosper—

he will join the generation of his fathers,

who will never see the light of life.

A man who has riches without understanding

is like the beasts that perish. (49:16-20)

Are you rich? You may not think you are, but in reality, you are amazingly rich. Not just in your financial wealth, but especially in your spiritual wealth as a Christian.

If you have traveled, you are well aware that most of the world can't imagine living like we do in America. In fact, my wife and I have made a point to send each of our four children on mission trips, for extended periods, to have their eyes opened to the reality of global existence. My kids will tell you that Dad has on more than one occasion exclaimed that the Garrison family lives like kings, for we do. This point is vividly made by Donella Meadows, a systems analyst and writer:

> If there were a representative global village of 1,000 people its principle make-up would be as follows: 584 would be Asians, 124

Africans, 84 Europeans, 84 Latin Americans, 55 from former Soviet nations, 52 North Americans and 6 Australians and New Zealanders. 329 would be Christians, 178 Muslims, 167 secularists, 132 Hindus, 60 Buddhists, 45 atheist, 3 Jewish and 86 claiming other affiliations. Out of the group of 1,000, 60 would receive half of the total income, 500 would be hungry, 600 would live in shantytowns and only 330 would have access to clean drinking water.

Since you are reading a book about leadership you probably are a leader, so you are likely better off than most folks. You probably have a higher level of education, position and influence than most. You no doubt have worked hard to attain the status you have achieved; however, don't let it go to your head.

A person with wealth, who lacks understanding, lives life like cattle (the Hebrew meaning for the word "beast" in verse 20). Ever watch a herd of cattle for any length of time? I grew up in northwest Indiana, so I've had my share of watching cattle. They really don't accomplish much in life other than graze, sleep and ultimately be killed for food. Of course, I don't really expect much from a "dumb animal" but we should and must from individuals with wealth.

The point of this passage isn't to criticize people with wealth, rather to remind them that having wealth is fleeting and can—and often does—influence one's worldview. God's Word is replete with warnings about the influence of money (Matthew 19:21-26; Mark 4:19; 1 Timothy 6:9-11; James 5:1-6).

King David's prayer from First Chronicles lays a powerful foundation for our attitude toward God's blessings and the things of this world:

> *Yours, O LORD, is the greatness and power*
>
> *and the glory and the majesty and the splendor,*
>
> *for everything in heaven and earth is yours.*
>
> *Yours, O LORD, is the kingdom;*
>
> *you are exalted as head over all.*
>
> *Wealth and honor come from you;*

you are the ruler of all things.

In your hands are strength and power

to exalt and give strength to all.

Now, our God, we give you thanks,

and praise your glorious name.

But who am I, and who are my people, that we should be able to give as generously as this? Everything comes from you, and we have given you only what comes from your hand. (I Chronicles 29:11-14)

Reflections on Leadership:

1. Make a journal entry concerning your status in life. Have you considered how blessed you are materially and spiritually? Has our culture oversold materialism to the populace? How has this materialistic mindset impacted your view of things and is it aligned with what Scriptures tell us is to be our attitude toward "things?"

2. Journal your thoughts on the following quotes on wealth:

    *   *"He is no fool who gives away what he cannot keep to gain what he cannot lose."* Jim Elliot, martyr and missionary to the Auca Indians

    *   *"Money never made a man happy yet, nor will it. There is nothing in its nature to produce happiness. The more a man has, the more he wants. Instead of its filling a vacuum, it makes one. If it satisfies one want, it doubles and triples that want another way."* Benjamin Franklin

#20: PROVERBS

Just Good Advice

The book of Proverbs is a "collection of collections" of some of the 3,000 proverbial statements (1 Kings 4:32) made by King Solomon. As you read this anthology, you will understand why Solomon was considered the wisest man who ever lived.

Since Proverbs is written in an almost scrapbook format, this leadership lesson will take a different form. Enjoy reading some of the wisest statements imaginable in order to lead well (Romans 12:8).

A Leader Should Fear God

> *The fear of the LORD is the beginning of knowledge, but fools despise wisdom and discipline.* (1:7)

This section on wisdom (Chapters 1-7) ends with a similar statement to what we find in this verse (Proverbs 7:2). Wisdom is assigned a feminine gender in the Hebrew language and depicts a woman calling out with a loud voice (Proverbs 8:1). The word "wisdom" has nothing to do with a person's IQ, rather their ability to learn and apply God's truth.

Why is fear the foundation for a person to receive wisdom? When you think about it, if a person is filled with pride, there is no respect for or desire to listen to God. In fact, the Bible tells us that a fool doesn't believe in God (Psalm 53:1). In a fool's mind, since God doesn't exist, what would he have to fear or learn from a non-existent deity?

Since you are a leader who believes in God and understands His nature (omnipotence, omnipresence and omniscience), you fear Him. The Hebrew word used in Proverbs 1:7 for "fear" is a word that literally means fear, terror or dread. Today, we don't like the idea of fearing God, but if we truly understand

God's nature, we should fear. Remember the God we are to fear is the God who calls us into intimacy, and orchestrated the plan to redeem a broken relationship through His Son. Our fear of God is just that, a fear of who He is, not a fear that keeps us from approaching Him through Christ.

A Leader Should Trust God

> Trust in the LORD with all your heart and lean not on your own understanding; in all your ways acknowledge Him, and He will make your paths straight. (3:5, 6)

This passage is often cited when you ask someone to quote Scripture. Frankly, I'm glad this is a popular passage, for it sums up how we are to live as Christians: trusting God. The world lives with the scientific method as its foundation—discounting the possibility that things unseen could be real—so it is unaware of another way to live. People of faith see God at work (making paths straight) regularly, but since God's work can't be put in a Petri dish and examined under a microscope, we are viewed as fools for Christ.

Leaders usually trust in themselves too much—am I wrong? Therefore, the admonishment to "lean not on your own understanding" can be a real challenge for some, but is necessary if we are to truly live a life of faith.

I will never forget writing a letter of resignation five years ago from my position as a college president. My wife and I had talked and prayed through the decision, but trusting God with our future was scary, especially when I was influenced by the poor economy and not knowing what the next step might be. The only thing I can tell you is that stepping out in faith and trusting God has been one of the most spiritually invigorating experiences in my life. Trust God, for He will astound you in the way He works.

A Leader Should Shun Fools

> He who walks with the wise grows wise, but a companion of fools suffers harm. (13:20)

The formula outlined in this verse is simple: If we associate with wise people, we gain their wisdom; if we associate with fools, we will take on their spirit.

I'm ashamed to admit it, but this verse has played out in my life. There have been times when those around me influenced my thoughts and words for the negative. As a father, I've often quoted 1 Corinthians 15:33 to my four children, *"Bad company corrupts good character."* A spiritually attuned leader will watch the company they keep—advice not just for our children, but for life.

A Leader Should Watch Their Words

When words are many, sin is not absent, but he who holds his tongue is wise. (10:19)

A gentle answer turns away wrath, but a harsh word stirs up anger. (15:1)

A fool finds no pleasure in understanding but delights in airing his own opinions. (18:2)

Some of you will remember Adlai Stevenson, who served as a U.S. Senator and was known as an outstanding orator. This quote comes from his experience in the use of words: "Man does not live by words alone, despite the fact that he sometimes has to eat them."

The third chapter of the book of James outlines our responsibility to watch our words and how we are to express words consistent with our faith. If you aren't familiar with this passage, James also contains a well know passage on the relationship between listening, speaking and anger:

Everyone should be quick to listen, slow to speak, and slow to become angry, for man's anger does not bring about the righteous life that God desires. (James 1:19b, 20)

A Leader Should Plan Accordingly

Plans fail for lack of counsel, but with many advisers they succeed. (15:22)

Commit to the LORD whatever you do, and your plans will succeed. (16:3)

Many are the plans in a man's heart, but it is the LORD's purpose that prevails. (19:21)

Make plans by seeking advice; if you wage war, obtain guidance. (20:18)

Here's an outline you can use in your planning:

1. Seek counsel.

2. Commit your plans to God.

3. Understand God is the one who determines the outcome.

Take this outline with you the next time you have a strategic planning session and see how others react to the notion that God is part of your company's plans. Most will mock the idea that God has anything to do with anything, let alone your business.

You might not have the freedom to share your faith in your company at the level you desire; however, as a biblical leader, you need to confess the influence of God in everything you plan in your business. God wants you to seek solid counsel, but He also wants you to admit that He is God and you aren't. Invite God into all your plans and expect Him to work in and through your life as a leader, to His glory.

Reflections on Leadership:

1. Review the following Scriptures on the fear of God and write your thoughts in your journal: Psalm 19:9; 34:11; 33:8; 86:11; Jeremiah 5:22; Ecclesiastes 12:13.

2. Trusting God isn't a concept to contemplate, rather something to act on. Review your life in Christ and remember the last time you trusted God and the circumstances that occurred through your trust. Are you in a situation right now where you need to trust God at a higher level? Write your reflections in your journal.

3. Acquaintances: Have you ever experienced the influence of foolish people in your life (1 Corinthians 15:33)? Why do you believe we sometimes are influenced by people that we don't want to emulate?

4. Planning: Consider the following quotes on planning and write your thoughts in your journal:

   • *"Plans are only good intentions unless they immediately degenerate into hard work."* Peter Drucker

   • *"In preparing for battle I have always found that plans are useless, but planning is indispensable."* Dwight Eisenhower

   • *"I know the plans I have for you," declares the LORD, "plans to prosper you and not to harm you, plans to give you hope and a future."* (Jeremiah 29:11)

#21: ECCLESIASTES

Work!

So I hated life, because the <u>work</u> that is done under the sun was grievous to me. All of it is meaningless, a chasing after the wind. I hated all the things I toiled for under the sun, because I must leave them to the one who comes after me. And who knows whether he will be a wise man or fool? Yet he will have control over all the work into which I have poured my effort and skill under the sun. This too is meaningless. So my heart began to despair over all my <u>toilsome</u> <u>labor</u> under the sun. For a man may do his <u>work</u> with wisdom, knowledge and skill, and then he must leave all he owns to someone who has not worked for it. This too is meaningless and a great misfortune. What does a man get for all the <u>toil</u> and anxious striving with which he labors under the sun? All his days his <u>work</u> is pain and grief; even at night his mind does not rest. This too is meaningless. (2:17-23)

If you read this passage out of context, it appears to be an indictment of work by the wisest man in history. However, if you continue reading (Ecclesiastes 2:24-26; 3:13; 5:18-20), you hear the "rest of the story" about work. Solomon saw great value in work:

Then I realized that it is good and proper for a man to eat and drink, and to find satisfaction in his toilsome labor under the sun during the few days of life God has given him—for this is his lot. (5:18)

During his reign as king, Solomon accomplished more than any of Israel's other kings and took a fledgling nation to the level of a world power. He wasn't afraid of work, but he realized that his hard work would be left to another, who didn't work for the inheritance and probably wouldn't appreciate the nature of work as he did. Yet, he knew that work was from God and could give a person great satisfaction and enjoyment.

The nature of work was forever changed by Adam and Eve's decision to disobey God: *"Cursed is the ground because of you; through painful toil you will eat of it all the days of your life. It will produce thorns and thistles for you, and you will eat the plants of the field"* (Genesis 3:17-18). I'm sure you have felt this curse on work during your career, yet work also gives mankind meaning and the resources for living. So, cursed or not, work is something that is part of our existence and is spoken of often in Scripture.

Today, it seems that many are dissatisfied with their work or have a lazy or entitlement mindset toward work. This mindset was humorously portrayed by the bohemian beatnik, Maynard G. Krebs in the early television program, *The Many Loves of Dobie Gillis* (1959-63). Maynard was played by Bob Denver (Remember: Gilligan of *Gilligan's Island?*) and expressed his attitude about work in the way he said, "WORK!" We laughed when we heard Maynard express his disdain toward work, but this attitude seems to have filtered into our culture.

As a leader, you probably get great satisfaction from your work. Your problem isn't that you dislike your work or are lazy; it is the need to find balance. Not the balance required to ride a bike but the balance in keeping life in perspective. The topic of balance is addressed in the book *The Juggling Act* by Dr. Pat Gelsinger. Gelsinger writes with candor about his struggles with balance and how work can morph from 9-5 to 24/7! Some of you are keenly aware that your life is imbalanced, and you want to gain the right perspective between faith, family, fun and work.

You know CEOs who have lost their perspective toward work. Working hard and smart are taught in Scripture (Proverbs 6:6; Ephesians 4:28b), but when our work consumes too much time and energy, it becomes an idol. Labeling work an idol is probably making some of you flinch, but the definition of an idol is *anything* that we place above God, and some leaders worship their work.

Our purpose with this leadership lesson isn't to demean the value of work, or to imply that there aren't those times in your work that extra time and energy are required, but balance should be the norm. Your faith adds another component to life that leaders without faith don't struggle with, but it is your faith that serves as a check and balance for life. Embrace faith's reminder that life is more than work, and our highest priority is our relationships. Our faith opened the door to a relationship with God that was closed by our sin; our faith defines love as selfless and patient; our faith defines the family and its function with one another; our faith tells us to work hard since it demonstrates our attitude of thankfulness to God; and our faith reminds us that work is accomplished in the context of community.

I'm not suggesting that balancing life is a simple formula of percentages allocated to each component; it is a daily decision to keep balance in relationships. Our highest relationship priority is to God since this will keep all other aspects of life in balance. If your life is out of balance, I guarantee that you are also struggling with your relationship with your Father. So, if balance is an issue, tomorrow provides the opportunity to begin the day with the Father, and He will put the rest of life into perspective.

Reflections on Leadership:

1. Is your life balanced (yes/no)? If your answer is yes, why do you think you are able to keep balance? If your answer is no, how are you out of balance?

    •   Has your spouse ever talked with you about balance in life? If so, what specific issues did they share? Have a discussion with your spouse about balance and write the points of the conversation in your journal. Write an action plan that you share with your spouse as to how you will bring balance into your life.

2. Write in your journal your reactions to the following quotes about work:

    •   *"All labor that uplifts humanity has dignity and importance and should be undertaken with painstaking excellence."* Martin Luther King, Jr.

    •   *"Far and away the best prize that life has to offer is the chance to work hard at work worth doing."* Theodore Roosevelt

#22: SONG OF SOLOMON

Love the One You're With

Lover

I liken you, my darling, to a mare

harnessed to one of the chariots of

Pharaoh.

Your cheeks are beautiful with

earrings,

your neck with strings of jewels.

We will make you earrings of gold,

studded with silver. (1:9-11)

Beloved

I am a rose of Sharon,

a lily of the valleys. (2:1)

When I started writing this book, taking a leadership lesson from each book of the Bible, I guess I forgot the enigmatic nature of Song of Solomon. Because this book is a challenge to interpret and deals with difficult, mature topics, it is often ignored in preaching.

Some believe this book should be viewed as an allegory (God is the bridegroom and the nation of Israel the bride of God), where others believe Song of Solomon should be seen as a typology, a type of Christ as He relates to the Church. Still others think the book should be interpreted in a natural or literal sense as a love poem of the love between Solomon and a young woman. Each of these views has some legitimacy in that there is a unique relationship between God the Father and Israel, Christ and His church, and a man and a woman. I'm interpreting the book as love poetry written early in Solomon's reign, for we are told in the sixth chapter he had 60 wives and 80 concubines when this book was penned. First Kings tells us that this number would swell to 700 wives and 300 concubines and these women would turn his heart (11:3, 4).

I'm sure none of you would read passages from Song of Solomon to your spouse to proclaim your love since the metaphors used are silly to moderns. However, one can appreciate this book since it represents a meaningful and passionate relationship between a ruler and a young commoner. We can only assume that this young woman became yet another of Solomon's escapades. Therefore, I'm not suggesting that we use Solomon as an example of a man who has his house in order as it relates to monogamous, lifelong marriage. In fact, his taking of many women reminds me of the 1970 song by Stephen Stills, *Love the One You're With*. Not God's design, nor did it play well in Solomon's life!

It is safe to say that most leaders are married. I believe it is also a truism that a leader who has a good marriage will be able to better focus on their work. I'm sure there are those who will read this leadership lesson and relate to the truth of my last statement. God designed marriage to be the most unique relationship on earth and it can be a leader's great source of joy and strength, or it can be the cause of pain and distraction.

Solomon's many wives and concubines led him down the path from being the wisest and most powerful man alive to becoming a man who wrote about the vanity of life. We see a radical change in his attitude from the book of Proverbs to the book of Ecclesiastes, and I believe much of this change of heart was caused by Solomon ignoring God's design in marriage.

Today, we live in a sexually charged and hedonistic world, where marriage is viewed as an antiquated concept in need of redefining. Christian leaders can also buy into the societal view of disposable marriages. Add power and money to the culture's influence, and Christian leaders can walk down the path to a ruined marriage.

As a godly leader, an authentic relationship with God will lead you to the next priority, that of guarding your marriage with your life. Yes, your life, because Paul reminds husbands to love their wives to the extent of laying down their lives for them, and wives to respect their husbands (Ephesians 5:21-33). Husbands and wives need to remember that Ephesians 5:21 asks that there be mutual submission, and that each have a wonderful role for a marriage to function.

Christian leaders can have a mistress—the mistress of work. As a leader, you probably receive more kudos at work for your leadership qualities than for being a great spouse and parent. Yet, as a person of faith, you know you should be known as a loving spouse and caring parent. So how can you keep your work in perspective with your family? Ask your spouse, and really listen to his or her answer. Then, talk with each of your children to see if they feel like second-class citizens in your kingdom.

Leader, your marriage requires your full attention and a high degree of energy, not the leftovers from a long, arduous day at work. If your marriage and home life are good, you will be a more effective leader, which is your desire in your role at work. However, if your home life is struggling, it will likely consume your mind and keep you from focusing on your work.

Since you love your work, you want to be the best leader you can be. One sure way of keeping that leadership edge is realizing the importance of your marriage and home life and leading in this arena of your life as well.

Reflections on Leadership:

1. Ask your spouse if they feel you are giving as much attention to the marriage and family as you do to your work. Be ready to hear his or her perspective. You may disagree with the evaluation, but it is his or her reality and therefore something you need to address.

    *   Ask the same question of your children. If your spouse and children tell you that you aren't giving enough attention to the family, discuss some simple ideas you could try to address this issue. You might need to seek professional assistance if you believe it can help deal with the issue of priority.

2. Write in your journal your thoughts to the following questions.

    *   Do you agree that your marriage and family life are important?

    *   Do you think you give as much energy and attention to your family life as to your work?

    *   If you give more attention to your work on a regular basis, why do you believe you do this?

3. Record your thoughts about the importance of marriage and family from the following quotes:

    *   *"The more you invest in a marriage, the more valuable it becomes."* Amy Grant

    *   *"A man should never neglect his family for business."* Walt Disney

#23: ISAIAH

The CEO of the Universe

In the year that King Uzziah died, I saw the LORD seated on a throne, high and exalted, and the train of his robe filled the temple. Above him were seraphs, each with six wings: With two wings they covered their faces, with two they covered their feet, and with two they were flying. And they were calling to one another:

> *Holy, holy, holy is the LORD Almighty;*
> *the whole earth is full of his glory. (6:1-3)*

Have you ever walked into a CEO's opulent office with a stunning view? Now imagine God's office (metaphorically speaking), from which He runs the Universe and be overwhelmed! Just imagine meeting the CEO of the universe and being awestruck by His power, knowledge and presence. This is the picture that the prophet Isaiah paints in this Scripture passage.

Isaiah's vision of God's throne room was given by God Himself, so there is a reason He gave this vision to the prophet. I believe the reason is a simple one: Mankind needs to be reminded who God is and stand in awe. Later in this passage, Isaiah writes his feelings about this vision and how it profoundly affected his life. I believe he was never the same after what he saw.

Mankind struggles with a universal problem—pride. I frankly don't know why we struggle with this, for in my life I've blown it enough times to keep me sufficiently humbled, yet pride still rears its ugly head again and again. Can you relate? We know that the sin of pride was at the core of Satan's rebellion and as the "prince of the earth," he seeks to influence us to live from a prideful perspective. Pride, according to the English Dictionary is an unreasonable conceit of superiority or overweening opinion of one's own qualities. Synonyms include: egotism, arrogance, hubris, vanity, boastfulness and self-centeredness.

As the first in the list of classical sins (pride, envy, anger, sloth, avarice, gluttony and lust) it can be argued that pride is the linchpin for other sins and something that Christian leaders must hold in check.

Unabashed pride is seen in the Garden of Eden when the newly created man and woman told God to buzz off with His rules and partook of the forbidden fruit. Pride was demonstrated by the nations building the Tower of Babel to reach God. King David showed incredible hubris toward God in taking another man's wife and having him killed to cover up his despicable actions. Pride is a heinous sin that elevates mankind to god status and removes God from His throne. Contrast these examples of pride gone wild with Christ's mindset of humility and servant-hood in Philippians 2:1-9.

Isaiah's description of God's appearance and throne room should serve as a vivid comparison between the Creator and the created. C.S. Lewis, in his essay, *The Great Sin* provides a modern comparison between mankind and God in the following quote:

> The Christians are right: it is Pride which has been the chief cause of misery in every nation and every family since the world began. Other vices may sometimes bring people together: you may find good fellowship and jokes and friendliness among drunken people or unchaste people. But Pride always means enmity—it is enmity. And not only enmity between man and man, but enmity to God.
>
> In God, you come up against something, which is in every respect immeasurably superior to yourself. Unless you know God as that— and, therefore, know yourself as nothing in comparison—you do not know God at all. As long as you are proud you cannot know God.

One of the greatest temptations for leaders is to allow pride to take a toehold and believe that they are better than others. A corner office, a jet at your disposal and a powerful position can cause a leader to believe he is better than others. Christian leaders can be drawn down the path of pride through their position, but Christians have the Bible to remind us that pride is a foundational sin and a Savior who exampled humility in life and demands the same of His followers.

Christian leaders should never live with pride as a regular part of their character profile. Rather, they should be humbled that God has selected them to lead and given them the stewardship of leadership. A prideful leader can't build a team, learn new lessons or accept feedback. Prideful leaders can't admit mistakes and never reach their potential because they have already arrived in their mind. Pride can be controlled through some simple measures, but only if you are willing to put these ideas into place.

- Look into the mirror of God's Word daily for it will do a great job of reflecting any pride in your life.

- Seek feedback from those you lead and your spouse: Give permission to those that know you best to demonstrate their love by telling you when they see pride in your life.

- Prayer and journaling: God's Spirit will bear witness with your spirit that pride resides in your life, so be open to God's Spirit in this area. Then, write in your journal about those scenarios where pride existed in your life and review your journal to see if you are seeing pride diminish.

This leadership lesson is one of the most important since I don't want to be the leader that God opposes because of my pride as outlined in James 4:6b.

> *God opposes the proud*
> *but gives grace to the humble.*

I want God's grace in my life, don't you? If you struggle with pride as a leader, then read Isaiah's vision of God over and over until you fall on your face before our Magnificent God: Get off His throne and let Him back in His rightful place.

Reflections on Leadership:

1. Take your direct reports to coffee and ask them if you come off as a person of pride. Make sure you listen and don't react to what you might hear. Then, do the same exercise with your spouse, for they know you better than any other person.

2. Write in your journal the following Scriptures and reflect on what they are telling you about the subject of pride:

    *   Psalm 73; Proverbs 8:13; 11:2; 16:5, 18-19; Isaiah 14:11-16; Philippians 2:1-9; James 4:6-10; 1 Peter 5:5-6; 1 John 2:15-16.

3. Read through the following quotes on pride and write in your journal what you believe God's Spirit is telling you about your pride.

    *   *"Yes, pride is a perpetual nagging temptation. Keep on knocking it on the head, but don't be too worried about it. As long as one knows one is proud, one is safe from the worst form of pride."* C.S. Lewis

    *   *"Good breeding consists of concealing how much we think of ourselves and how little we think of the other person."* Mark Twain

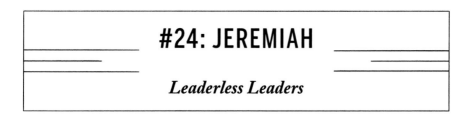

#24: JEREMIAH

Leaderless Leaders

So I will go to the <u>leaders</u>

and speak to them;

surely they know the way of the LORD,

the requirements of their God."

But with one accord they too had <u>broken off the yoke</u>

<u>and torn off the bonds</u>. (5:5)

There's a reason Jeremiah is known as the "weeping prophet" for he was asked by God to deliver a message of judgment to Judah because of their apostasy.

Has a nation ever changed its gods?

(Yet they are not gods at all.)

But my people have exchanged their glorious God

for worthless idols. (2:11)

There is tremendous irony that the godless nation of Babylon would be God's instrument of destruction. Babylon was not God's chosen people, so when Israel determined to forsake God, they would be destroyed by a nation whom they felt a moral superiority to, yet when they "changed gods," they opened themselves up to God's wrath in whatever form it would take.

The passage cited from the fifth chapter is part of a longer passage (5:1-6) where Jeremiah was asked to find one person in Judah who lived truth. No such person was found, so Jeremiah approached the leaders of Judah thinking that they would see the nation's apostasy. Judah's leaders failed to demonstrate truth in their lives and *broke off the yoke and tor off the bonds of the LORD*. A leader by definition is one who has commanding authority or influence (*Merriam-Webster Dictionary*), so when a leader fails to influence for the good, they are worthless or "leaderless leaders." How tragic it is when a person is given the mantle of leadership and fails to lead, yet this is exactly what we find in Jeremiah's day.

A leader's motive should never be to seek a position of influence without understanding the responsibility that goes along with the role, yet, history is filled with illustrations of just such scenarios. Some leaders seek a leadership role because of the power, money and influence of the position, rather than use the position for good. This perspective is the antithesis of what godly leaders are called to demonstrate. We are called to exercise our God-given skills with humility and with a goal of serving those we lead. What a stark contrast with many leaders who lead from self-seeking ambitions.

One of the greatest examples of a man who led in a time of moral morass is William Wilberforce (1759-1833). Wilberforce was a British parliamentarian and philanthropist who struggled with his political life, believing that ministry was more important. Today, we are thankful that men like John Wesley challenged Wilberforce to remain in the thick of the parliamentarian fight to abolish slavery from the British Empire.

> Wilberforce's first inclination after his conversion to faith in Christ was to leave the world of politics and be ordained as a minister— mistakenly believing, as many do, that spiritual things are higher than secular things. Fortunately, friends counseled him to stay and discover his calling in public life. John Newton and Thomas Scott, for example, were two ministers who wisely persuaded him to serve in Parliament and not become a minister. (From *The Life of William Wilberforce*, a biography by his son, Samuel)

Wilberforce lived in a day when slavery was viewed as morally acceptable, yet after his conversion he was compelled by his faith to fight slavery since he now viewed it as a great moral evil. His lifelong fight for abolition would be completed only days before his death.

William Wilberforce faced the great evil of his day, slavery. Why didn't the leaders of Judah see the evil of apostasy in their day and devote their leadership influence in turning their nation toward God? I believe the secret is found in the war between living a life of *convenience versus conviction*. Wilberforce shares his conviction through a journal entry from September 28, 1787.

> God Almighty has set before me two great objects, the suppression of the Slave Trade and the reformation of manners.

Leaders can be caught up in living a life of comfort and missing the opportunity to serve as an instrument of good. Today, the temptation for leaders to live a life of convenience is pervasive, but godly leaders can't ignore the mandate they have to serve as catalysts for good in their sphere of influence.

One of Wilberforce's friends wrote about the dangers of fighting against slavery. His statement serves as a vivid reminder that leading against the evil of the day might cost a leader the ultimate price—life!

> I shall expect to read of you being carbonadoed by West Indian planters, barbecued by African merchants and eaten by Guinea captains, but do not be daunted, for—I will write your epitaph!

Reflections on Leadership:

1. The days of Jeremiah were filled with the evil of apostasy. What evils do you see in our day, and have you ever used your leadership position to influence for godliness? What was the cost of using your influence for good?

2. Reflect in your journal about the following quotes on facing evil:

    *   *"He who passively accepts evil is as much involved in it as he who helps to perpetrate it. He who accepts evil without protesting against it is really cooperating with it."* Martin Luther King Jr.

    *   *"It's better to be good than evil, but one achieves goodness at a terrific cost."* Stephen King

#25: LAMENTATIONS:

A Tough Assignment

The LORD has brought her grief because of her many sins.
Her children have gone into exile, captive before the foe. (1:5)

All the splendor has departed from the Daughter of Zion.
Her princes are like deer that find no pasture. (1:6)

Her filthiness clung to her skirts; she did not consider her future.
Her fall was astounding; there was none to comfort her. (1:9)

"The Lord has rejected all the warriors in my midst; he summoned an army against me to crush my young men. In his winepress the Lord has trampled the Virgin Daughter of Judah." (1:15)

"This is why I weep and my eyes overflow with tears. No one is near to comfort me, no one to restore my spirit." (1:16a)

This book's name says it all—*Lamentations!* The root of lamentation is lament: to wail, express sorrow or regret. Imagine being given the assignment of writing a lament for a nation that fell from greatness. This is the assignment God gave to Jeremiah.

Old Testament prophetic books have a monolithic theme: Israel turns their back on God and is judged. Lamentations was written from Jerusalem and describes a great city and nation that lost its way and is the shadow of its former glory. The secret to blessings seems so simple: If Israel honored and obeyed God, it would be blessed. Then why is this simple concept so difficult to achieve? This is a rhetorical question since the nature of mankind is to reject God's authority and, therefore, stay on the merry-go-round of rejection and judgment.

Our topic in this leadership lesson concerns itself with the nature of mankind, for our Scripture is about a nation that lost its battle with evil. Robert Louis Stevenson wrote about this struggle between good and evil in the *Strange Case of Dr. Jekyll and Mr. Hyde* (1886). In this classic piece of English literature we read a quote that describes the struggle between good and evil in fallen mankind.

> It was the curse of mankind that these incongruous personalities—the good and the bad were thus bound together—that in the agonized womb of consciousness, these polar twins should be continuously struggling.

The Apostle Paul in the book of Romans provides a vivid description of the good and evil that war with one another in our flesh.

> *So I find this law at work: When I want to do good, evil is right there with me. For in my inner being I delight in God's law; but I see another law at work in the members of my body, waging war against the law of my mind and making me a prisoner of the law of sin at work within my members. What a wretched man I am! Who will rescue me from this body of death? Thanks be to God—through Jesus Christ our Lord.* (Romans 7:21-25)

The Bible is a book about our sin. Yes, my sin and yours, for we have all have missed the mark of God's bull's-eye of perfection. Paul again writes about this struggle in a letter to the church at Ephesus.

> *As for you, <u>you were dead in your transgressions and sins, in which you used to live when you followed the ways of this world and of the ruler of the kingdom of the air, the spirit who is now at work in those who are disobedient</u>. All of us also lived among them at one time, gratifying the cravings of our sinful nature and following its desires and thoughts. Like the rest, we were by nature deserving of wrath. But because of His great love for us, <u>God, who is rich in mercy, made us alive with Christ</u>*

even when we were dead in transgressions—it is by grace you have been saved. (Ephesians 2:1-5)

I underlined two parts of this passage to demonstrate how we used to think and live, and then how God's grace energized our spirit, forgave us our sins and gave us a new orientation for life. Therefore, believers should never expect mankind to live as if they have the benefit of faith.

Frankly, I can't understand why most people in the world believe that mankind is good, yet that is exactly what they believe. Somehow, we bought into the lie that, as we become more educated, economically prosperous or create great technologies, we are becoming a virtuous people. From my perspective, God's Word describes mankind's nature as sinful and reflects reality more accurately than the philosophical pundits.

Since man's nature is sinful, Biblical leaders should consider the implications of this truth. Leading people who have a sin nature, as well as coping with one's own sin, exacerbates the work of leading. It might help in our leading in a fallen world to keep the following in mind:

1. Don't expect those you lead to reflect a Christian spirit in their beliefs, words or actions.

2. Do lead with words and actions that reflect your faith so that those you lead have the opportunity to see faith in action.

3. Do share your faith when the opportunity comes from a life well lived and consistent with Christian teaching.

4. Do pray for those who you come in conflict with in the business world understanding that they don't have the insight that faith in Christ provides, yet they desperately need it.

Reflections on Leadership:

1. Write about the following questions in your journal:

    *   If you have felt frustration in leading, have you considered why leading people is so challenging?

    *   Do you consider your leadership position an opportunity to live and share your faith? If so, how have you lived and shared your faith in the marketplace?

2. The following quotes are about a lack of leadership, so reflect on how they might relate to your leadership.

    *   *"The day soldiers stop bringing you their problems is the day you have stopped leading them. They have either lost confidence that you can help them or concluded that you do not care. Either case is a failure of leadership."* Colin Powell

    *   *"Don't measure yourself by what you have accomplished, but by what you should have accomplished with your ability."* John Wooden

#26: EZEKIEL

Leaders as Watchmen

After seven days the LORD gave me a message. He said, "Son of man, I have appointed you as a <u>watchman</u> for Israel. Whenever you receive a message from me, warn people immediately." (3:16, 17)

When the <u>watchman</u> sees the enemy coming, he sounds the alarm to warn the people. Then if those who hear the alarm refuse to take action, it is their own fault if they die. They heard the alarm but ignored it, so the responsibility is theirs. If they had listened to the warning, they could have saved their lives. But if the <u>watchman</u> sees the enemy coming and doesn't sound the alarm to warn the people, he is responsible for their captivity. They will die in their sins, but I will hold the <u>watchman</u> responsible for their deaths. (3:16,17; 33:3-6) NLT

The term "watchman" is one of those antiquated terms we can't relate well to in our era of video cameras and high tech surveillance monitoring. We can't imagine a day when someone was needed to watch for an enemy attack. Few of us has ever lived in a walled city where watchmen are on constant vigil looking for an approaching threat. Watchmen were very important in Ezekiel's day; they were the eyes and ears of a city that protected its inhabitants.

Ezekiel was living in Babylon, along with many of his countrymen from Judah when he wrote this book about events that took place in Jerusalem from 593-573 B.C. Many of the events can be dated with pinpoint accuracy, in some cases to the actual day they occurred.

Judah had hoped to hear good news from their prophet that would indicate that they would return to their beloved land. However, the news they received was not good, for Ezekiel was taken back to Jerusalem through a God-given vision that would tell of this city's destruction (586 B.C.). God instructs

Ezekiel to serve as a watchman several times in this book. In each case, the watchman told of Judah's sin and an approaching enemy that would destroy their capital city. The watchman metaphor is used with several other prophets in the Old Testament, all with the message of God's judgment: Isaiah 56:10; Jeremiah 6:17; Hosea 9:8.

As I considered the idea of Ezekiel serving as a watchman, it seemed clear that all leaders must serve as watchmen. Two terms come to mind in considering leaders as watchmen: vigilant and strategic.

- **Vigilant:** This word is defined as being alert and watchful, especially to avoid danger. A leader must be a person of vigilance in scouring the landscape for threats that could impact their business or ministry. Watchman leaders can never rest from this task. Even when they are away from the city wall, they must assign the task to those who will take the watch seriously.

- **Strategic:** Strategic comes from the Greek word *strategia* and means the office of general command. A military leader is strategic in planning the details of a conflict. A leader as a watchman must also be strategic in seeing the threat, noting what direction it comes from and framing actions to overcome the enemy.

Today, leaders don't stand on parapet walls. They are watching through reading, talking with others who can help give them new or fresh perspectives, listening with care and taking the time to assimilate all input. Godly leaders can add to their watchman work the power of God's Word and His Spirit to give godly insight as well as spiritual interpretation of the surroundings.

Serving as a watchman isn't glamorous work, for it is many lonely days of just watching. The days of watching must be coupled with both vigilance and strategies to communicate and address the threat. It is work that must be done 24/7 and may go on year after year without ever seeing a threat, but being prepared for when a threat comes, for threats will come in every leader's tenure.

Leader, climb high on the wall of the city to gain a different perspective of what might be heading your way. Perspective is important, but being able to see and identify the threat are best understood using spiritual insight gained through time with God, seeking His strength, vision and wisdom.

Reflections on Leadership:

1. Review the following Scriptures which talk about the work of watch-men and write your thoughts in your journal: 2 Samuel 18:24-27; 2 Kings 9:17-20; Psalm 127:1; Isaiah 62:6; Jeremiah 6:17.

2. Evaluate how you have acted as the watchman at your business or ministry. Have you demonstrated vigilance and strategic thinking in the way you have led the business or ministry you oversee? Write in your journal your evaluation of how you are serving as a watchman as well as how you can improve this aspect of your leadership.

3. Review the following quotes that pertain to vigilance and strategy and write your thoughts in your journal.

    *   *"Eternal vigilance is the price of liberty."* Thomas Jefferson

    *   *"I claim not to have controlled events, but confess plainly that events have controlled me."* Abraham Lincoln

#27: DANIEL

A Leader's Leader

Now, Belteshazzar [Daniel], tell me what it means, for none of the wise men in my kingdom can interpret it for me. But you can, because the spirit of the holy gods is in you. (4:18b)

There is a man in your kingdom who has the spirit of the holy gods in him. In the time of your father he was found to have insight and intelligence and wisdom like that of the gods. (5:11)

It pleased Darius to appoint 120 satraps to rule throughout the kingdom, with three administrators over them, one of whom was Daniel. The satraps were made accountable to them so that the king might not suffer loss. Now Daniel so distinguished himself among the administrators and the satraps by his exceptional qualities that the king planned to set him over the whole kingdom. (6:1-3)

Do you know anyone who is viewed as a leader's leader because they distinguish themselves through their leadership? Such leaders are few and far between, but it is safe to say that Daniel was such a leader.

The book of Daniel contains some of the most recognized passages in the Bible. However, it needs some context to best understand the environment that Daniel faced as a leader.

Daniel and many of his countrymen were carried off to Babylon in 605 B.C. as part of the Jewish Diaspora. Daniel's writings were probably designed to serve as a source of encouragement from God even in the midst of desperate days of exile.

Babylon came to be a powerful nation through the Amorite king, Hammurabi, but lost much of its power after his death. This nation came again into greatness under Nebuchadnezzar's (Nabopolassar's son) leadership. Nebuchadnezzar ushered in a time of expansion and building—the Hanging Gardens of Babylon are an illustration of the magnificent building during this period (one of the Seven Wonders of the Ancient World). Babylon had a powerful military and economic strength, but it was a nation of moral wickedness.

It was in this context that Daniel found himself. Yet, even in this evil culture, Daniel lived and worked in such a way that showed that he was unique from other leaders in Babylon. Daniel became an interpreter of dreams and God's spokesman to those in leadership (Nebuchadnezzar, Belshazzar [Nabonidus' son and co-regent]).

Daniel continued to influence Persian leaders (another powerful and wicked nation) after they overcame Babylon during Darius and Cyrus' reign. It was during these days that Daniel and his friends were most challenged to recant their faith when jealous Persian leaders pushed to pass a law that punished those who worshipped any god or man other than Darius. It seems apparent that Darius missed how such a ruling would impact Daniel, a man for whom he had great respect (Daniel 6:14-28).

There is no question that Daniel demonstrated stellar character qualities and competency at a level not often seen in leaders. He found himself in leadership positions in a godless nation; subservient to men who had no respect for his God, yet he led in such a way to propel him to the front of other leaders. What was it about this leader that made him a leader's leader? The best way to answer this question is from Scripture: *They could find no corruption in him, because he was <u>trustworthy</u>* (Hebrew: *aman*) *and <u>neither corrupt</u>* (Hebrew: *shechath*) *nor <u>negligent</u>* (Hebrew: *shalu*) (Daniel 6:4b). The emphasized words are powerful words in the context of leadership. To use a well-known idiom, Daniel was "ahead of the curve" as a leader because he was trustworthy, without corruption or negligence. Let's take each of these words and define them so we can better understand the power of such ideals as a leader.

- Trustworthy: defined as worthy of confidence, dependable; synonyms: reliable, responsible, tried-and-true

- (without) Corruption: defined as an impairment of integrity, inducement to wrong by improper or unlawful means; synonyms: decay, putrescence, decadence

- (nor) Negligent: defined as failure to exercise the care that a reasonable prudent person would exercise in life circumstances; synonyms: dereliction, laxness, remissness, slackness

Daniel was a leader who could be implicitly trusted; a man you knew would never do anything improper and always get the job done. You can clearly see that a leader who exemplifies such characteristics would rise to the top.

Over 35 years ago I had the honor of working in the administration of LeTourneau University, which R. G. LeTourneau founded in 1946, to help GIs returning from the war gain skills for industry. During my time at the university I watched dozens of films about his earth moving equipment, reviewed files he kept on the messages he presented at thousands of churches and spoke with his personal assistant about his life and impact. If you want to read more about this amazing leader I suggest you read, *Mover of Men and Mountains*. LeTourneau is probably known best for living on 10 percent and giving away 90 percent while living a life of trustworthiness, integrity, and passion for his work.

Dare to be a Daniel leader in a world that has seemingly has forgotten what makes a leader's leader: trustworthiness, integrity and passion for your work.

Reflections on Leadership:

1. Take your journal and write an epitaph of what people say about your leadership. Does your epitaph contain characteristics like follow-through, above reproach, trusted, what you see is what you get?

2. If your epitaph unearths weaknesses in your character, what is your plan to correct these shortcomings in your leadership? Write your plan of attack in your journal and share your plan with an accountability partner.

3. Consider the following quotes and write your thoughts in your journal as to how they apply to your life:

    *   *"In looking for people to hire, you look for three qualities: integrity, intelligence, and energy. And if they don't have the first, the other two will kill you."* Warren Buffet

    *   *"A person who is fundamentally honest doesn't need a code of ethics. The Ten Commandments and the Sermon on the Mount are all the ethical code anybody needs."* Harry. S. Truman

#28: HOSEA

You Want Me To Do What?

When the LORD began to speak through Hosea, the LORD said to him, "Go, marry a promiscuous woman and have children with her, for like an adulterous wife this land is guilty of unfaithfulness to the LORD." So he married Gomer daughter of Diblaim, and she conceived and bore him a son.

Then the LORD said to Hosea, "Call him Jezreel, because I will soon punish the house of Jehu for the massacre at Jezreel, and I will put an end to the kingdom of Israel. In that day I will break Israel's bow in the Valley of Jezreel."

Gomer conceived again and gave birth to a daughter. Then the LORD said to Hosea, "Call her Lo-Ruhamah, for I will no longer show love to the house of Israel, that I should at all forgive them. Yet I will show love to the house of Judah; and I will save them—not by bow, sword or battle, or by horses and horsemen, but by the LORD their God." (1:2-7)

"Lord, you want me to do what? With every fiber within me, I don't want to marry Gomer, but I know that you are asking me to do this to make a point. What was the point again?"

Can you imagine what was going through Hosea's mind when he was asked to marry Gomer? She was an adulterous woman who would give birth to children with strange names like, Jezreel (God sows), Lo-Ruhamah (she is not loved) and Lo-Ammi (not my people). Strange names, but these names expressed God's frustration with the Northern Kingdom of Israel, for they had forsaken the Lord through their worship of other gods and disobedience to God's law. Prophets were Old Testament leaders asked to do difficult things for God Almighty. They were preachers (Jonah 3:4), predictors of coming events (1

Samuel 3:19) and watchmen (Ezekiel 3:17). Their assignments caused their lives to be lonely—communicating hard news, challenging others to see impending disaster and carrying out other crazy assignments. You might be thinking how this sounds a lot like your leadership position.

Let's look at some possible parallels in the lives of all leaders:

1. Difficult assignments: You probably won't be asked to marry an adulterous woman, but you may well be asked to do things that are difficult, like moving when you just moved last year, taking a division that has lost money for years and the board expects you to turn it around in a year or working with others who would love to see you fail so they can move up the corporate ladder. With each difficult assignment you must ask yourself if the assignment is worth what it will demand and how it may take your life out of balance.

2. Preacher: You're probably not a seminary graduate, but as a Christian leader you are a preacher. A preacher is one who proclaims the truth of Scripture. As a Christian leader you have a calling to proclaim God's truths as they relate to the way business should be run (with integrity) and how people are to interact with one another. Yes, you are a preacher in the marketplace, what better pulpit?

3. Predictor: This aspect of leadership is a natural for leaders, but Christian leaders should keep in mind that they have insight that most don't— their eyes of faith. You must read the journals and trade publications to keep abreast of what's happening in your business, but your eyes of faith can help you see the world through a different lens: a lens that sees people as at the very heart of God.

4. Watchman: I wrote about the idea of leader as a watchman in leadership lesson #26 from the book of Ezekiel. When one thinks of watchmen, one thinks of a person of vigilance and strategy. As a Christian leader you can't afford to be lazy in this aspect of leading. You must stand at the wall of the city with your eyes scanning the horizon for possible

attackers and think strategically as to how to cope with the attacks that come your way as a leader.

Hosea was asked to do something no leader desires, but because of his passion for and understanding of God, he took the assignment, knowing it would benefit many, while denying self.

Reflections on Leadership:

1. In your journal reflect on the difficult assignments you have been given in your tenure as a leader. What was your reaction when you were given the challenging assignments, and what did you learn through them?

2. Have you ever been asked to do something that you felt you couldn't or shouldn't do and decided to turn down the assignment? Why did you turn the assignment down, and what was the outcome of this situation?

3. Consider the following quotes on leadership challenges and write your reactions in your journal:

   - *"If your actions inspire others to dream more, learn more, do more and become more, you are a leader."* John Quincy Adams, 6th American President

   - *"Your time is limited, so don't waste it living someone else's life. Don't be trapped by dogma—which is living with the results of other people's thinking. Don't let the noise of others' opinions drown out your own inner voice. And most important, have the courage to follow your heart and intuition. They somehow already know what you truly want to become. Everything else is secondary."* Steve Jobs

#29: JOEL

What in the World is Sackcloth?

Put on sackcloth, O priests, and mourn;

wail, you who minister before the alter.

Come, spend the night in sackcloth,

you who minister before my God;

for the grain offerings and drink offerings

are withheld from the house of your God.

Declare a holy fast;

call a sacred assembly.

Summon the elders

and all who live in the land

to the house of the LORD your God,

and cry out to the LORD. (1:13-14)

Sackcloth. What in the world is that? It's the last thing you would want next to your skin! Originally used in making sacks, it is the coarse, rough, thick hair of goats and is used in the Bible as a symbol of repentance or mourning. In Genesis 37:34, Jacob wore sackcloth when Joseph disappeared; David dawned this coarse cloth at Abner's death in 2 Samuel 3:31; and Mordecai covered himself in sackcloth when he heard of the impending persecution of his people (Esther 4:1, 2). Joel was a prophet to the Southern Kingdom of Israel, and his assignment was to call his people to repentance. Little is known about Joel, but his name means Jehovah is God (appropriate for a prophet). The book of Joel tells about God's judgment by an unimaginable infestation of locusts, but it also describes future judgment by the term, the "Day of the Lord."

The prophet Joel showed great leadership in calling the priests and elders to repent of their country's sin. Leaders have the role of "convening" (definition of convene: to summon, to assemble) people and groups for a purpose. Joel's purpose was to call to repent, but leaders can convene for many reasons.

You probably haven't thought about your leadership role as one of convening, but it is one of the most important things you do. In my role as the president of a college, I brought many groups together, and I set the agenda and tone of those gatherings. There were times when I brought faculty and staff together because there was an attitude or action that needed to be confronted because it was causing conflict in our college community.

Most leaders want to be liked, but leadership isn't about being liked, it's about ensuring that a business or ministry is heading in the right direction. This implies the need to confront and correct through convening people and leading them in the process of bringing the ship back on course.

Be it a nation, a business or a ministry, leaders must understand one of their primary roles is to convene or gather people together. In his book *Community: The Structure of Belonging,* Peter Block states that every time a leader convenes people, it is an "opportunity." An opportunity for the leader to state the purpose of the gathering and to help those gathered understand the goals and direction they are headed.

Effective convening requires <u>courage</u>, <u>purpose</u> and <u>skill</u>. Some leaders have a difficult time convening groups, so they miss the opportunity to impact the business. It takes courage to bring people together, especially when the purpose is a difficult one. Convening also must have a stated purpose, even if it is to celebrate. Some of the skills needed whenever you convene include using clear methods to communicate the purpose, and developing a means to evaluate whether the purpose was understood. If you believe that each time you convene groups you are performing one of the most important roles as a leader, you will always take the time to prepare. I suggest taking a note card and writing out a simple plan that lists those who will be present, the meeting's purpose(s) and finally how you will communicate the purpose.

Reflections on Leadership:

1. To convene means to have courage, purpose and skill. Have you demonstrated courage when you needed to correct or confront people or groups that were taking the business off course? Write in your journal an evaluation of your courage coefficient (scale 1 - 5: 1 means "I can't confront"; 5 means "I'm confronting too often"). Also, write about a situation when you failed to confront and another situation when you did confront an issue that required your attention and how each scenario turned out. What could you learn about convening from this assignment?

2. After reading the following quotes, write in your journal how you might use them to help you better bring people together for a common purpose:

    *   *"I have a different vision of leadership. A leader is someone who brings people together."* George W. Bush

    *   *"Leadership begins with understanding that every gathering is an opportunity to deepen accountability and commitment through engagement."* Peter Block, author of *Community: The Structure of Belonging*

#30: AMOS

Bad Business

Hear this, you who trample the needy

and do away with the poor of the land, saying

"When will the New Moon be over

that we may sell grain,

and the Sabbath be ended

that we may market wheat?"

Skimping on the measure,

boosting the price

and cheating with dishonest scales,

buying the poor with silver

and the needy for a pair of sandals,

selling even the sweepings with the wheat. (8:4-6)

In the cited passage, we see that businessmen as far back as the 8th century B.C. used unscrupulous business practices. In this case, the wrongdoing was taking advantage of the poor by using dishonest scales. This goes against God's standard of accurate measurements (e.g. talent, shekel, cubit and homer) outlined in Leviticus 19:35-36:

Do not use dishonest standards when measuring length, weights or quantity. Use honest scales and honest weight, an honest ephah and an honest hin. I am the LORD your God, who brought you out of Egypt.

Scales in Biblical times lent themselves to dishonest standards, since they were primitive devices, and the standards for weights were somewhat subjective. The shekel, which means "to weigh," equals .41 ounces, but archaeologists have discovered differing amounts that range from .41 to .35 ounces. Such a small variance seems insignificant, but it becomes significant as product amounts increase.

Other passages in the Bible speak to dishonest scales, such as Micah 6:11. In this passage it appears that the businessman is using weights that appear to be correct but are inaccurate. This same idea of false measurements is described in Malachi 3:8-10, where God accuses some of lying about the amount of food they brought to His storehouse.

Lying about the value of something reminds us of the story of Ananias and Sapphira in Acts 5. This couple was involved in a real estate deal with good intentions. They sold their property with the intent of giving the proceeds to their church, but when Ananias gave a different amount from the sale price, Peter asked him why he lied. Apparently, this couple collaborated about their story, because Sapphira repeated the same amount of the sale as her husband. In this case, their bad business practices brought untimely death. We are told that their deaths reverberated through the fledgling church (Acts 5:5) and certainly were deterrents from similar practices.

Amos calls out businessmen who are using faulty scales, but bad business practices can take on a plethora of forms. A business leader can allow bad business practices through false financial statements, shortcuts in manufacturing that knowingly impact the quality of a product, slow or non-payment of a supplier or breaking the terms of a contact. You no doubt can add to the list from personal experience, but I pray you have never been the leader who allowed bad business practices on your watch.

Forbes, and the Ethisphere Institute, a New York City think tank, have for the past five years assembled a list of the World's Most Ethical Companies. The latest list was compiled from nearly 3,000 companies, in 100 countries and 36 industries. Ethisphere has created a proprietary rating system, called Ethics Quotient. Selection is done by reviewing the following:

- Codes of ethics

- Litigation and regulatory infraction history

- Investment and business practices

- Nominations of senior executives for leadership excellence

- How industry peers, suppliers and customers view the company

As followers of Christ, the companies or ministries you oversee should exemplify places of integrity and good business practice and be viewed as companies worthy of being listed among the world's most ethical. It should never be said of you or your company that you were unscrupulous. The following Scriptures from Job and Titus clearly teach we are to live lives above reproach:

> *And the LORD said to Satan, "Have you considered My servant Job, that there is none like him on the earth, a blameless and upright man, who fears God and turns away from evil? He still holds fast to his integrity, although you incited Me against him to destroy him without reason." (Job 2:3)*

> *Show yourself in all respects to be a model of good works, and in your teachings show integrity, dignity and sound speech that cannot be condemned, so that an opponent may be put to shame, having nothing evil to say about us. (Titus 2:7-8)*

Reflections on Leadership:

1. Reflect back through your career. Have you ever seen or been part of any business practice that was dishonest or lacked integrity? Journal about that experience and draw insights into how you found yourself in that situation. What were your actions before, during and after this bad business scenario?

2. Read the following quotes about good and bad business practices and record your thoughts in your journal.

    *   *"At this moment, America's highest economic need is higher ethical standards—standards enforced by strict laws and upheld by responsible business leaders."* George W. Bush

    *   *"Try not to become a man of success, but rather try to become a man of value."* Albert Einstein

#31: OBADIAH

Pride Goes Before a Fall

The vision of Obadiah.

This is what the Sovereign LORD says about Edom—

> *We have heard a message from the LORD:*
>
> *An envoy, was sent to the nations to say,*
>
> *"Rise, and let us go against her for battle"—*
>
> *"See, I will make you small among the nations;*
>
> > *you will be utterly despised.*
>
> *The <u>pride</u> of your heart has deceived you,*
>
> > *you who live in the clefts of the rocks*
> >
> > *and make your home on the heights,*
>
> *you who say to yourself,*
>
> > *'Who can bring me down to the ground?'*
>
> *Though you soar like the eagle*
>
> > *and make your nest among the stars,*
> >
> > *from there I will bring you down,"*
>
> *"In that day," declares the LORD, "will I not destroy the wise men of Edom, men of understanding in the mountains of Esau?"* (1-4, 8)

Our leadership story from Obadiah is about the pride of Judah's neighbors to the south, the Edomites. These people are descendants of Esau (Genesis 25:30) and the focus of the book of Obadiah and God's judgment.

Jerusalem was destroyed in 586 B.C., and many of Judah's neighbors supported the Babylonians in their quest to take this capital city. Our Scripture passage tells us that the Edomites were secure in their rocky stronghold (v. 3), in self-sufficiency (vv. 2-4) and in their wisdom tradition (v. 8). Yet, none of these were enough to withstand the impending doom from the hand of the Lord. The Edomites give meaning to the idiom, "Pride goes before a fall."

The Hebrew word for pride in Obadiah 1:3 is *zadon*, which describes a state or condition of an inflated attitude of oneself, or overconfidence to the point of moral failure. This same word is used in the book of Proverbs in less than flattering ways:

> *Pride leads to disgrace, but with humility comes wisdom.* (Proverbs 11:2)

> *Pride leads to conflict; those who take advice are wise.* (Proverbs 13:10)

> *Mockers are proud and haughty; they act with boundless arrogance.* (Proverbs 21:24)

Pride is at the top of the classical list of vices and it can be argued that it is the foundation of other vices (pride, envy, anger, sloth, avarice, gluttony and lust). Synonyms for pride carry the same ugly implication, be it hubris, ego, vainglory or haughtiness. The Bible records that pride was Satan's great sin (Isaiah 14:12-14) and those who follow after him demonstrate this same character flaw (1 Timothy 3:6). Each vice has its contrasting virtue. Pride's opposing virtue is humility and is described as part of the mind of Christ (Philippians 2:7, 8). It can be safely said that pride could become a leader's Achilles' heel if not kept in check. It seems that pride can often be proportionate to a person's possessions, position of power and level of education. I'm not saying that a person with such things will be prideful, only that there is likelihood. This likelihood is greatly diminished if the person is willing to have others speak truth into their lives, or sets parameters in life to keep themselves from becoming prideful. One must be proactive with the cancerous mindset of pride and cut it out as soon as it becomes evident.

America's first president, George Washington, was a leader who apparently understood the nature of pride and kept it in check. The distinguished historian, James Thomas Flexner, best known for his four-volume biography on Washington, says much about Washington's character in the following quote: "I found a great and good man. In all history, few men who possessed unassailable power have used that power so gently and self-effacingly for what their best instincts told them was the welfare of their neighbors and all mankind."

Toward the close of the Revolutionary War, Washington lived with his troops, took no salary and refused to take leave to Mount Vernon. In some cases, the troops had not been paid in many years. In this context, some encouraged Washington to use his power and proclaim himself "George I of the United States" and lead a coup against Congress. Washington could have easily taken the path of other leaders who allowed power to corrupt their character.

Pride does go before a fall. This phrase is more than a well-known idiom, it is the number one reason leaders fail. As a Christian leader, you must build into your life anything that keeps you grounded to understand who you are in Christ. You are unique in all Creation, but called to lead with the mind of Christ . . . humility.

Reflections on Leadership:

1. What have you done that allows others permission to tell you that you appear prideful? If you haven't built into your life those checkpoints, what will you do from this point forward to help keep your pride in check? Write out your plan and share it with those you give permission to tell you about your pride.

2. Read the following quotes on pride and leadership and record your thoughts in your journal.

   • *"Humility is to make a right estimate of one's self."* Charles H. Spurgeon, well-known British preacher of the 19th century

   • *"A proud man is always looking down on things and people; and, of course, as long as you're looking down, you can't see something that's above you."* C. S. Lewis

#32: JONAH

Open Mouth, Insert Prophet

The word of the LORD came to Jonah, son of Amittai; "Go to the great city of Ninevah and preach against it, because its wickedness has come up before me."

But Jonah ran away from the LORD and headed for Tarshish. (1:1-3)

But Jonah had gone below deck, where he lay down and fell into a deep sleep. (1:5b)

"I am a Hebrew and I worship the LORD, the God of heaven, who made the sea and the land." (1:9)

"Pick me up and throw me into the sea," he replied, "and it will become calm, I know that it is my fault that this great storm has come upon you." (1:12)

From inside the fish Jonah prayed to the LORD his God. He said:

"In my distress I called to the LORD and he answered me." (2:1-2a)

Then the word of the LORD came to Jonah a second time: "Go to the great city of Nineveh and proclaim to it the message I give you." (3:1)

Jonah obeyed the word of the LORD and went to Nineveh . . . He proclaimed: "Forty more days and Nineveh will be overturned." (3:3, 4)

He prayed to the LORD, "O LORD, is this not what I said when I was still at home? That is why I was so quick to flee to Tarshish, I know that you are a gracious and compassionate God, slow to anger and abounding in love, a God who relents from sending calamity. Now, O LORD, take away my life, for it is better for me to die than to live." (4:1b-3)

129 ◇ 129 ◇

Don't be too hard on Jonah. You and I have done the same things we criticize him for through our leadership. Well, haven't we? Have we ever disobeyed, run away from God or been less than compassionate about a person or group? We condem Jonah for his actions and use him as the ultimate example of a leader who disobeyed God. We also love the creative way God deals with Jonah: Open the great fish's mouth and insert disobedient prophet!

The Lord's assignment for Jonah was the last thing he wanted to hear. He hated the inhabitants of Nineveh and wanted God's judgment, not grace. His feelings for Nineveh were grounded on facts, not just perception.

Jonah (c. 782-753 B.C.) prophesied during the reign of Jeroboam II (2 Kings 14:25). Assyria was Israel's sworn enemy and Nineveh was that nation's capital. So when the Lord told Jonah to go to Nineveh, a city of ruthless people who had killed many of Jonah's countrymen, Jonah was repulsed at the thought of God's grace being extended to such people. Historians tell us that the Assyrians are viewed as some of the most brutal warriors in the history of warfare. They kept extensive records of their conquests, which tells us something about how they felt about war and overcoming other nations.

Maybe an analogy will help us understand Jonah's distain for the Assyrians. Almost 420,000 Americans died during World War II. If you were an American asked to minister in Germany in 1946, I'm sure you would struggle with your feelings and possibly turn down such an assignment.

If you can't relate to events of 70 years ago, maybe you can relate to a business competitor who defamed your character to one of your major clients, or a CFO who embezzled funds from your company. You are asked to reconcile with these people who have hurt you to your very core. How do you feel about making up with those who have sought your harm?

We typically view this book from Jonah's vantage point, but we also need to analyze the story through God's eyes. God wanted to extend His grace through the message of repentance by His prophet to an undeserving people. Remember that God had negative feelings for the Assyrians as well, since they had caused great sorrow to His people, Israel. Why would God desire an evil people to repent and enjoy His grace? Because it is God's nature to extend His grace to undeserving people. Sound familiar? Remember when you heard the Gospel for the first time? That you had sinned, that God's Son was crucified for your sin and that Christ arose from the dead to overcome the penalty of sin. In confession and acceptance of God's grace, you were made right with God and adopted into His family (Ephesians 1:3-5). Another passage in Ephesians makes God's grace crystal clear:

> *As for you, you were dead in your transgressions and sins, in which you used to live when you followed the ways of this world and of the ruler of the kingdom of the air, the spirit who is now at work in those who are disobedient. All of us also lived among them at one time, gratifying the cravings of our sinful nature and following its desires and thoughts. Like the rest, we were by nature objects of wrath. But because of his great love for us, God, who is rich in mercy, made us alive with Christ even when we were dead in transgressions—it is by grace you have been saved.* (Ephesians 2:1-5)

I'm not trying to downplay Jonah's disobedience, but I want to remind us that we can be like Jonah in not wanting God to extend mercy and grace to those who have hurt us. Jonah's enemies had hurt his countrymen in unimaginable ways, yet God wanted Nineveh to have the opportunity to repent of their wrongdoings. In this book we see them repenting, but Nahum prophesized their demise, which occurred when an alliance of Medes, Babylonians and Scythians destroyed Nineveh in 612 B.C.

As leaders, I'm sure you have been hurt by those you thought were friends, or those who intentionally wanted to hurt you. That's the nature of leadership—others will hurt you from time to time. But, the difference in Biblical leaders is to forgive those who have hurt you (the Ninevites in your life) and extend mercy and grace for their wrong. If you allow your feelings for those who have hurt you to thrive, then who is being impacted? You! You are the one being manipulated by your ill-will for another rather than experiencing the freedom of forgiveness. I can't help but remember the day I experienced God's forgiveness and grace when at the age of 15, I heard the Gospel. God's forgiveness changed the direction of my life that day.

Reflections on Leadership:

1. In your journal write the names of those who have hurt you during your leadership career. Examine your mind and heart concerning the names you have written. Have you forgiven those who hurt you? If not, why haven't you been able to forgive? What actions will you take to move toward forgiveness?

2. Read the following quotes and write your thoughts in your journal:

    •   *"Forgiveness is a gift you give yourself."* Suzanne Somers

    •   *"Forgiveness is the remission of sins. For it is by this that what has been lost, and was found, is saved from being lost again."* Saint Augustine

#33: MICAH

Don't Be So Naive

Woe to those who plan iniquity,

to those who plot <u>evil</u> on their beds!

At morning's light they carry it out

because it is in their power to do it.

They covet fields and seize them,

and houses, and take them.

They defraud a man of his home,

a fellowman of his inheritance. (2:1, 2)

The prophet Micah prophesized during the reign of kings Jotham, Ahaz and Hezekiah, which places his ministry alongside those of Isaiah, Amos and Hosea. Prophets served as the mouthpiece of God to Israel and Judah. Micah proclaims God's judgment upon Judah (3:1-4, 4:10a) and focuses on what the "evil" people do to one another. As I read the cited passage from Micah, I was reminded that we are seeing something unimaginable happen in our day. Most people don't believe there is evil, even with the enormity of evidence that it does exist.

In 1973, Dr. Karl Menninger wrote a fascinating book called *Whatever Became of Sin*. In this book, Dr. Menninger discusses how our culture has systematically cleansed the idea of sin from our way of thinking: "In all the laments and reproaches made by our (modern day) seers and prophets, one misses any mention of sin, a word which used to be a veritable watchword of

(Old Testament) prophets. It was a word, once in everybody's mind, now rarely, if ever heard. Where indeed did sin go? What became of it?"[1]

Clearly, our cited Scripture tells us there are people who enjoy plotting and carrying out their evil plans. Scripture is replete with examples of the reality of evil, but none describes evil better than Ephesians 6:10-17 :

> *Finally, be strong in the Lord and in his mighty power. Put on the full armor of God so that you can take your stand against the devil's schemes.* <u>*For our struggle is not against flesh and blood, but against the rulers, against the authorities, against the powers of this dark world and against the spiritual forces of evil in the heavenly realms.*</u> *Therefore, put on the full armor of God, so that when the day of <u>evil</u> comes, you may be able to stand your ground, and after you have done everything, to stand. Stand firm then, with the belt of truth buckled around your waist, with the breastplate of righteousness in place, and with your feet fitted with the readiness that comes from the gospel of peace. In additional to all this, take up the shield of faith, with which you can extinguish all the flaming arrows of the evil one. Take the helmet of salvation and the sword of the Spirit, which is the word of God.*

Sin and evil are themes throughout the Bible. "The Biblical story has four unique chapters: Genesis 1-2 and Revelation 21-22. These chapters are unique in that no sin is present in the places and events described."[2] Evil is real, and we face its manifestations daily through our personal interactions. Realizing that evil exists is something all leaders must confess, and they must think and act knowing that people are born with a sin nature.

Leaders, don't be so naïve. You are surrounded by people who epitomize the cited Scripture. They plan their evil and execute it with glee, seeing how their words and actions destroy others. These people don't know any better since their spirit is dead and unable to consider the truths of Scripture. We must also keep ourselves from being deceived by those who proclaim faith and are deceitful

---

1. p.13
2. Craig VanGelder, *The Essence of the Church* [Grand Rapids: Baker Books, 2000], 89

in their actions. These individuals have learned this tactic from Satan, who masquerades as an angel of light (2 Corinthians 11:14). I was a freshman in high school when the first *Star Trek* episode was aired. *Star Trek's* creator, Gene Roddenberry, believed that as education and technology advanced, they would eliminate mankind's ills, concepts he wrote into most episodes. However, in the ensuing years, with all of the available educational options and technological advances, we haven't seen mankind grow less evil. In fact, the 20th century was the deadliest in history, and the 21st century is on track for being even more so. Clearly, evil isn't eradicated when education and technology increase!

Evil was never more evident than during World War II, when 50-70 million people died at the hands of evil. Pastor Dietrich Bonhoeffer, who was hung for his collaboration to kill Hitler, wrote from prison his thoughts on evil in *Letters and Papers from Prison*:

> Here and there people flee from public altercation into the sanctuary of private virtuousness. But anyone who does this must shut his mouth and his eyes to the injustice around him. Only at the cost of self-deception can he keep himself pure from the contamination arising from responsible action. In spite of all that he does, what he leaves undone will rob him of his peace of mind. He will either go to pieces because of this disquiet, or become the most hypocritical of Pharisees.

> Who stand fast? Only the man whose final stand is not his reason, his principles, his conscience, his freedom, or his virtue, but who is ready to sacrifice all this when he is called to obedient and responsible action in faith and exclusive allegiance to God—the responsible man, who tries to make his whole life an answer to the question and call of God. Where are these responsible people?

Reflections on Leadership:

1. Take your journal and consider the following Scriptures that speak about evil in the world. Did you believe that evil was real before reading these Scriptures? Has your understanding of evil changed through reviewing these verses?

   • Proverbs 2:6-13; Isaiah 5:20-21; Matthew 7:15-23; Luke 6:45; Romans 16:17-18.

2. Reflect on your leadership career and recall a situation when evil was most evident. Consider the following questions about that situation:

   • Who manifested an evil motive or actions in this story?

   • What was the manifestation of evil (words, actions and/or attitude)?

   • How was this situation addressed and rectified, if it was?

   • What did you learn from this experience, and how have you applied this lesson to other evil situations since?

3. Read the following quotes on the nature of evil and record your thoughts in your journal:

   • *The spread of evil is the symptom of a vacuum. Whenever evil wins, it is only by default: by the moral failure of those who evade the fact that there can be no compromise on basic principles.* Ayn Rand, author

   • *"The world is a dangerous place to live; not because of the people who are evil, but because of the people who don't do anything about it."* Albert Einstein

#34: NAHUM

Beware Lest You Fall

You have increased the number of your merchants
till they are more than the stars of the sky,
but like locusts they strip the land
and then fly away.
Your guards are like locusts,
your officials like swarms of locusts
that settle in the walls on a cold day—
but when the sun appears they fly away,
and no one knows where.

O king of Assyria, your shepherds slumber,
your nobles lie down to rest.
Your people are scattered on the mountains
with no one to gather them.
Nothing can heal your wound,
your injury is fatal.
Everyone who hears the news about you
claps his hands at your fall,
for who has not felt
your endless cruelty? (3:16-19)

As I read this Scripture passage regarding God's judgment on Assyria (612 B.C.), I was reminded of another passage that refers to another judgment of God—1 Corinthians 10:12:

> *So, if you think you are standing firm, be careful that you don't fall!*

This verse should be understood in the context of Numbers 25:9, where we read about God's judgment on Israel through a plague, which killed 24,000 men because they had committed sexual sin with Moabite women and worshipped Baal.

In our 32nd leadership lesson from the book of Jonah, we heard how the Ninevites (Assyrians) repented of their wrongdoings and were spared judgment. Fast-forward 100 years to Nahum's day and we read about Assyria's impending destruction. The Assyrian destruction was through an alliance of Medes, Babylonians and Scythians and was so complete that their capital city, Nineveh, was never rebuilt and was covered by wind-blown sand. Historians knew virtually nothing about Assyria until archeologists, excavating Tell Kuyunjik in 1949, found Sennacherib's palace and 22,000 cuneiform clay tablets that told the story of this super power.

What happened between the repentance in Jonah's day to the forecast of judgment in Naham's day? We are given some idea in the cited passage from the book of Nahum:

- Assyrian business owners had multiplied exponentially through their many military conquests of other nations and had stripped the resources of the conquered people for Assyrian causes.

- Assyrian officials (political leaders) had also multiplied in number and were lazy and worthless by failing to lead their people.

- Assyrian leaders (business and political) were known for their many cruelties to the nations they defeated.

These three bullet points can be best understood in the context of alliteration: *motive, motivation* and cruel *manifestations*.

What was the primary *motive* of the Assyrian business leader? I believe it was greed, since the metaphor of locusts stripping the land is used to describe their actions. Greed is a theme often discussed in Scripture and is best understood from this passage from Luke 12:13-21:

> *Someone in the crowd said to him, "Teacher, tell my brother to divide the inheritance with me."*
>
> *Jesus replied, "Man, who appointed me a judge or an arbiter between you?" Then he said to them, "Watch out! <u>Be on your guard against all kinds of greed; a man's life does not consist in the abundance of his possessions.</u>"*
>
> *And he told them this parable: "The ground of a certain rich man produced a good crop. He thought to himself, 'What shall I do? I have no place to store my crops.'"*
>
> *"Then he said, 'This is what I'll do, I will tear down my barns and build bigger ones, and there I will store all my grain and my goods. And I'll say to myself, 'You have plenty of good things laid up for many years. Take life easy; eat, drink and be merry.'"*
>
> *"But God said to him, 'You fool! This very night your life will be demanded from you. Then, who will get what you have prepared for yourself?'"*
>
> *"This is how it will be with anyone <u>who stores up things for himself but is not rich toward God.</u>"*

Greed is the theme of Greek mythology's *King Midas* or Ebenezer Scrooge from Dickens' *A Christmas Carol.* It reminds us that one's perspective can be perverted by the unending pursuit of possessions. All leaders, be they kings, business owners or ministry heads need to maintain a constant vigil to keep a balance between the "things of life" versus the "relationships of life." Abiding in Christ (John 15) helps frame a godly mindset in the way we relate to others and the things of the world, where an absence of abiding opens our heart up to mistreating others and to personal greed.

The second problem with Assyrian political leadership concerned their *motivation*, or lack of it. There is nothing more disturbing than to see a leader who fails to perform the duties of leadership. Romans 12:8 contains a list of spiritual gifting and lists leadership as a spiritual gift that must performed "diligently."

An antiquated word for laziness is sloth, certainly not a word understood in our day. Sloth was one of the *Classical Sins* and is best defined by the author of this classification, Thomas Aquinas: "Sloth is a sluggishness of mind which neglects to begin good . . . (it) is evil in its effect, if it so oppresses man as to draw him away entirely from good deeds."

The Bible speaks often to the subject of physical laziness, but the outward manifestation of laziness comes from a misunderstanding of our motive in our work:

> *Whatever you do, work at it <u>with all your heart</u>, as <u>working for the Lord</u>, not for men, since you know that you will receive an inheritance from the Lord as a reward. <u>It is the Lord Christ you are serving</u>.* (Colossians 3:23, 24)

Finally, the Assyrian leaders were known for their cruel *manifestations*. The definition of cruel is one who inflicts pain or suffering and is devoid of humane feelings.

What a triumvirate of leadership wrongdoings these Assyrian business and political leaders demonstrated. Yet, today's leaders must evaluate if they have shown any measure of greed, sloth or cruel actions or mindset through their leadership.

Biblical leaders aren't perfect by any measure, but what we do have is the constant reminder in God's Word that godly leaders are to be markedly different from godless leaders. Following are some reflections to help you look at your leadership in the mirror of God's standard. Beware, lest you fall as a leader and lead like an Assyrian.

Reflections on Leadership:

1. With your journal before you, reflect on your career to determine if greed, laziness or cruel actions or attitudes toward others have manifested themselves in your life. If so, write out the details of these times with the intent of seeking God's insight into how such things could enter into your life when your desire is to be a godly leader.

2. Reflect and write your thoughts on the following quotes on greed, laziness and cruelty:

   • *"It has always seemed strange to me... the things we admire in men, kindness and generosity, openness, honesty, understanding and feeling, are the concomitants of failure in our system. And those traits we detest, sharpness, greed, acquisitiveness, meanness, egotism and self-interest, are the traits of success. And while men admire the quality of the first they love the produce of the second."* John Steinbeck

   • *"Human nature is above all things lazy."* Harriet Beecher Stowe

#35: HABAKKUK

Why?

Habakkuk's Complaint:

>*Why do you make me look at injustice?*
>
>*Why do you tolerate wrong?*
>
>*Destruction and violence are before me;*
>
>*there is strife, and conflict abounds.*
>
>*Therefore the law is paralyzed,*
>
>*and justice never prevails.*
>
>*The wicked hem in the righteous,*
>
>*So that justice is perverted.*

The LORD's Answer:

>*Look at the nations and watch—*
>
>*and be utterly amazed.*
>
>*For I am going to do something in your days*
>
>*that you would not believe,*
>
>*even if you were told.*
>
>*I am raising up the Babylonians,*
>
>*that ruthless and impetuous people,*
>
>*who sweep across the whole earth*
>
>*to seize dwelling places not their own.* (1:3-6)

Why does God allow evil to prevail? Have you ever asked this question? Well, then you can imagine the frustration Habakkuk felt when he realized that God heard his prayer for justice but would use the wicked Babylonian nation to judge his homeland, Judah.

This book is yet another Old Testament book that outlines judgment upon Judah for their sins. If you remember your Bible history, the King of Judah during Habakkuk's time is the wicked king put in power by the Egyptians, Jehoiakim (2 Kings 23:36-24:6). His father was Jehoahaz, who lasted only three months before being defeated by an invading army from Egypt. The sad part of this story is the fact that the king prior to Jehoahaz was his father, the godly King Josiah. Thus, in a very short period of time the nation of Judah went from knowing the blessings of God to being overthrown and living in idolatry. Leadership is everything in the life of a nation, for as its leaders go, so goes the country.

We find Judah poised for yet another invasion, this time by a "ruthless and impetuous people" (1:6), the Babylonians. Habakkuk was told in verse 5 to get ready to be "utterly amazed" by what God was going to do. What the Lord was planning to do in judgment of Judah was truly dumbfounding to this prophet—using a wicked superpower to mete out His wrath.

So why would the Lord use a more wicked nation to overthrow Judah, His chosen nation? Judah had fallen into yet another season of idolatry and the prophet Habakkuk was pleading for judgment on his own people. This fact tells us how utterly wicked Judah had become under Jehoiakim. The Lord was going to use a wicked nation to judge another wicked nation, but He would not stop there. He would ultimately bring judgment on Babylon (539 B.C.) for their wrongdoings.

Somehow, Habakkuk had fallen into the trap of comparing evil with evil. His own country (less evil than Babylon in his eyes) had a less than stellar history of following God. In fact, it can be argued that Judah was blessed with the opportunity to see God at work, and yet decided time and again to turn their back on the Lord. So, God in His sovereign understanding of all things, decided to use "a more evil nation" to bring judgment on Judah.

One might remember this same viewpoint by another prophet, Jonah. He felt that Nineveh didn't deserve an opportunity to repent, because they were too evil. It is a matter of perspective. The nation of Israel was chosen to carry the seed of the Savior, but when they failed to live up to this royal responsibility, they too would be judged for their sins. Why then did Israel think that their sins were somehow less evil in God's eyes than another nation's?

At this point, I'd like to confront our nation, America, because somehow we have lost our perspective regarding our sin and the way we compare ourselves to other nations' sins. I believe that this nation has demonstrated in its brief history a high standard when it comes to helping and protecting other peoples, but we have also somehow lost sight of how evil we have become in our modern day debauchery and profound materialism. Somehow, we have lost our perspective of what we were and how to honor God as a nation.

Our lessons on leadership have attempted to focus on the impact a leader can have on those they lead, so let's transition this lesson to the individual leader. Have you ever felt like Habakkuk, in that you wanted God's judgment on those evildoers that surround you? Have you ever questioned how your desired judgment on evil was ignored or improperly administered? Here is the gist of this book. There are times when judgment is administered through the constructs of man and can be questioned as to the nature or form of man's judgment, for mankind can judge with an imperfect judgment. However, there are times when God divinely intervenes in a situation—as God did by using Babylon to judge Judah—and administers His perfect judgment. God's judgment doesn't always fit our understanding of perfect judgment, but rest assured it is, for it is God's judgment. It might help to consider how some of your decisions and judgments as a leader can be misunderstood by those you lead. How can they not understand why you made a certain decision? The problem is one of perspective. As a leader you have a vastly different understanding of situations into which you inject your judgment. You have access to information that most don't, so naturally you make decisions from a greater understanding. So too, God has an understanding of people, nations and history that dwarfs our limited vantage point. I can't imagine in my wildest dreams what God knows, so too, I will have a difficult time understanding the way He might judge. My role as a Biblical leader is to trust His working in my life (although I'm sometimes dumbfounded) and be reminded that those I lead sometimes need help understanding my judgments. It's a matter of perspective.

Reflections on Leadership:

1. Through your years in leadership, have you ever been misunderstood by direct reports, employees or others that didn't understand why you made a particular decision? Why do you believe this misunderstanding existed? Was the misunderstanding one of perspective, or some other reason? Write your thoughts in your journal.

2. Consider the following quotes on judgment and write your thoughts in your journal:

   - *"Do not wait for the last judgment. It comes every day."* Albert Camus

   - *"And I saw something else under the sun: In the place of judgment—wickedness was there, in the place of justice—wickedness was there. I thought in my heart, "God will bring to judgment both the righteous and wicked, for there will be a time for every activity, a time to judge every deed."* (Ecclesiastes 3:16, 17)

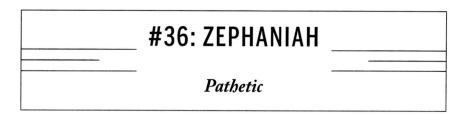

#36: ZEPHANIAH

Pathetic

Woe to the city of oppressors,

rebellious and defiled!

She obeys no one, she accepts no correction.

She does not trust in the LORD,

she does not draw near to her God.

Her <u>officials within her</u>

<u>are roaring lions</u>;

her <u>rulers are evening wolves</u>,

who leave nothing for the morning.

Her <u>prophets are unprincipled</u>;

they are treacherous people.

Her priests profane the sanctuary

and do violence to the law. (3:1-4)

The backdrop of this book is similar to other minor prophets; Judah isn't following God and will be judged. Assyria is at its pinnacle of power and Judah's king, Amon, has led an unsuccessful revolt against the Assyrian king, Ashurbanipal. Judah was soundly defeated, Amon was killed and an eight-year-old king, Josiah, would be placed in power. During Josiah's reign (640-609 B.C.) he would initiate many reforms after the Book of the Law was discovered during repairs to the temple (2 Kings 22:8-13). However, Zephaniah was written before these reforms were enacted during a time of religious indifference, injustice and economic greed (Zephaniah 1:4-13; 3:1-4, 7). Judah's officials, rulers and prophets were pathetic and miserably inadequate. Imagine being described as roaring lions, evening wolves and unprincipled; but those are exactly the terms God used for Judah's leaders.

The book of James also provides a New Testament reminder that leaders can set a pathetic example:

> *Now listen, you rich people, weep and wail because of the misery that is coming upon you. Your wealth has rotted, and moths have eaten your clothes. Your gold and silver are corroded. Their corrosion will testify against you and eat your flesh like fire. You have hoarded wealth in the last days. Look! The wages you failed to pay the workmen who mowed your fields are crying out against you. The cries of the harvesters have reached the ears of the Lord Almighty. You have lived on earth in luxury and self-indulgence. You have fattened yourselves in the day of slaughter. You have condemned innocent men, who were not opposing you. (5:1-6)*

What an indictment to these business leaders who took advantage of those they used in their journey to wealth, for they were acting like those described in Zephaniah—roaring lions and evening wolves.

We often hear about leaders who use their positions of power and influence for personal gain, and take advantage of others in their quest for power and money. I understand how power and money can corrupt a leader and lead them down the path of self-centeredness and greed (1 Timothy 6:6-10; 1 John 2:15, 16), but this should never happen in the life of a Christian leader. The only way Christian leaders can take the pathetic road of hubris is if they don't allow others to hold them accountable when they drift from a godly path.

Rather than write a leadership lesson on the pathetic leadership in Zephaniah's day, I'd like to transition our thinking to great leadership. Previously I mentioned James Thomas Flexner's seminal work on George Washington, *Washington: The*

Indispensable Man. The following quote from Flexner's introduction sums up Washington's leadership during America's foundational days:

> Beginning thus, as it were anew, I found a fallible human being made of flesh and blood and spirit—not a statue of marble and wood. And inevitably—for that was the fact—<u>I found a great and good man. In all history few men who possessed unassailable power have used that power so gently and self-effacingly for what their best instincts told them was the welfare of their neighbors and all mankind.</u>

Note how Flexner described Washington: a great and good man, and a man who used his power gently, yet was aware of his competence as a leader (self-effacing). Stories about Washington's faith abound, and apparently his faith was real, because it manifested itself in his leadership. History tells us that Washington could have moved the presidency into a monarchy, but his character and understanding of power and leadership allowed him to walk away from a throne.

Washington's leadership is the description of a leader who understood leadership principles from Scripture. The following verses remind us how Christian leaders are to lead:

> *Now Moses was a very <u>humble man</u>, more humble than anyone else on the face of the earth.* (Numbers 12:3)

> *And David shepherded them with <u>integrity of heart</u>; with skillful hands he led them.* (Psalm 78:72)

> *Do <u>nothing out of selfish ambition or vain conceit</u>, but in <u>humility</u> consider others better than yourselves. Each of you should look not only to your own interests, but also to the interests of others. Your attitude should be the same as that of Christ Jesus: Who, being in very nature God, did not consider equality with God something to be grasped, but made himself nothing, taking the very nature of a servant, being made in human likeness.* (Philippians 2:3-7)

Judah's pathetic leadership is a vivid reminder that leaders can easily be swayed from the path of Biblical leadership. Therefore, Christian leader, be aware that you can move off course without the inspiration of Scripture. Also, invite trusted confidantes to speak truth into your life, thus assuring accountability to your leadership.

Reflections on Leadership:

1. What are you currently doing to ensure that your leadership doesn't move down the path to pathetic leadership? Evaluate your current discipline of reading and meditating on Scripture and how you allow others to give input into your leadership. Journal your thoughts on this reflection question.

2. Read and write your thoughts on the following quotes on poor and good leadership:

    *   *"Nothing so conclusively proves a man's ability to lead others as what he does from day to day to lead himself."* Thomas J. Watson, former CEO of IBM

    *   *"A good leader is a person who takes a little more than his share of the blame and a little less than his share of the credit."* John Maxwell

#37: HAGGAI

First Things First

In the second year of King Darius, on the first day of the sixth month, the word of the LORD came through the prophet Haggai to Zerubbabel son of Shealtiel, governor of Judah, and to Joshua son of Jehozadak, the high priest.

This is what the LORD Almighty says: "These people say, 'The time has not yet come for the LORD's house to be built.'"

Then the word of the LORD came through the prophet Haggai. "<u>Is it a time for you yourselves to be living in your paneled houses, while this house remains a ruin?</u>"

Now this is what the LORD Almighty says: "<u>Give careful thought to your ways. You have planted much, but have harvested little. You eat, but never have enough. You drink, but never have your fill. You put on clothes, but are not warm. You earn wages, only to put them in a purse with holes in it.</u>"

This is what the LORD Almighty says: "Give careful thought to your ways. Go up into the mountains and bring down timber and build the house, so that I may take pleasure in it and be honored," says the LORD. "<u>You expected much, but see, it turned out to be little. What you brought home, I blew away. Why?" declares the LORD Almighty. "Because of my house, which remains in ruin, while each of you is busy with his own house.</u>" (1:1-9)

Then Haggai, the LORD's messenger, gave this message of the LORD to the people: "I am with you," declared the LORD. So the LORD stirred up the spirit of Zerubbabel son of Shealtiel, governor of Judah, and the spirit of Joshua son of Jehozadak, the high priest, and the spirit of the whole remnant of the people. *They came and began to work on the house of the LORD Almighty, their God, on the twenty-fourth day of the sixth month in the second year of King Darius.* (1:13-15)

Haggai is one of the shortest books in the Old Testament, but it contains 25 proclamations that the prophet's message was directed by the Lord. The book's message is directed toward the nation of Judah and its theme is to motivate the people to finish the temple of God. No doubt Haggai was anxious to see the temple completed since he remembered Solomon's temple and its glory. The temple's foundation was completed 16 years earlier, but since then, the people deviated from their assignment, instead building for themselves fancy paneled houses ("paneled houses" in 1:3 might have also meant that they simply had a roof).

"First things first" is a well-known idiom, but it is also the name of a book by Stephen Covey (*First Things First*, 1994) on time management. An idiom about priority and a book about time management fits nicely into Haggai's theme since it is about priorities. The best definition for priority is "something given or meriting attention before competing alternatives." This fits perfectly with Judah's decision to forego completing the temple and building their homes instead.

Part of me wants to cut Judah some slack in building their homes. After all, they had just returned to Jerusalem from exile and needed somewhere to live. Historians tell us that the Persian king, Cyrus the Great, allowed some 50,000 Jews to return to Judah under Zerubbabel's leadership to complete the temple. Judah apparently took this assignment seriously since we know they finished the foundation within two years (Ezra 3:8-13).

Imagine, you were in exile, living as slaves and the outcasts of another culture, and you now find yourself back in your own country and have worked hard for two years to complete the foundation. What would be wrong with building a place to live before completing the temple? Their thinking seems logical if it weren't for the fact that their first priority was to complete the temple. The people's thinking was convoluted on several levels: First, they were to finish the temple before anything else; and second, their intent of finishing the temple after their homes was completely forgotten, since they hadn't done anything after completing the foundation 16 years earlier!

Some commentaries tell us one of the possible reasons they didn't return to completing the temple is because they used all the accessible wood in building their homes (Haggai 1:7, 8). The foundation was an easy chore since it was made of stones, that were available from the ruins of the previous temple that was destroyed by the Babylonians in 586 B.C. Judah apparently heeded the warning of God through His prophet to complete the temple, for it was finally completed in 515 B.C.

God sure seems like an exacting taskmaster with His assignments, doesn't He? The Bible is replete with examples of challenging assignments: Joseph being sold in slavery, wrongly accused and imprisoned so that he might ultimately be elevated to the number two leader in Egypt and save a nation, and Christ's assignment to leave his rightful place in Heaven to be born in poverty and experience an unimaginably horrible death as our sin sacrifice! Anytime you think your assignment is a tough one just remember these examples.

This leadership lesson is about priority and so I was reminded of the first question of the *Westminster Catechism,* which addresses the question of priority:

> **Q.** What is the chief end of man?
>
> **A.** Man's chief end is to glorify God (1 Corinthians 6:20), and to enjoy (Philippians 4:4) Him forever.

What a great question and answer. Indeed, our first priority in life is to glorify God and enjoy His invitation to love Him and be loved in relationship. This answer makes so much sense, yet I'm sure many of the readers of this lesson struggle with setting it as a foundational priority. From this foundation of giving glory and enjoying God, we are given specific assignments as we live out our life to glorify Him.

I have the honor of interacting with many business leaders across the country and I would say that the number one issue that I hear from them is that of balance. Life comes at leaders fast and furious, so it is extremely easy to allocate too much of life to things that aren't meant to be priorities. I'm sure you have heard the following illustration about a teacher who placed a large empty jar on his desk and placed large rocks into the jar to the top. He then asked the rhetorical question if the jar was as full as it could be. Taking smaller rocks, he was able to place many smaller rocks among the large rocks, and again asked if the jar was full. Next he added sand to the jar, which allowed him to fill every crevasse. He again asked if the jar was full. Finally, he took some water, which filled areas in the jar the small gains of sand weren't able to reach. "Now," he stated, "the jar is as full as it can be." This jar illustration can be understood in the context of priorities in life. The large rocks represent the real priorities of life: love of God, family and others (Matthew 22:37-40). The smaller rocks are also important, like career or school, and finally the sand and water represent the myriad of other things we allow in life. Ironically, we don't always see how our life's priorities shift from the important, to building paneled houses for ourselves.

God's priorities in life are to glorify Him and enjoy Him, so always remember to "keep the main thing the main thing" (Stephen Covey).

Reflections on Leadership:

1. Reflect over your leadership career and recall a time when your life was lived out with the right priorities, and then a time when you had lost balance. Which time was the best and why?

2. Read the following quotes on priority and write your thoughts in your journal:

    *   *"It is not an arrogant government that chooses priorities; it's an irresponsible government that fails to choose."* Tony Blair

    *   *"The will of God is not something you add to your life. It's a course you choose. You either line yourself up with the Son of God... or you capitulate to the principle which governs the rest of the world."* Elisabeth Elliot

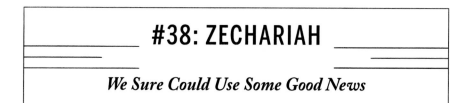

#38: ZECHARIAH

We Sure Could Use Some Good News

So he said to me, "This is the word of the LORD to Zerubbabel: 'Not by might nor by power, but by my Spirit,' says the LORD Almighty."

"What are you, mighty mountain? Before Zerubbabel you will become level ground. Then he will bring out the capstone to shouts of 'God bless it! God bless it!'"

Then the word of the LORD came to me: "The hands of Zerubbabel have laid the foundation of this temple; his hands will also complete it. Then you will know that the LORD almighty has sent me to you.

"Who dares despise the day of small things, since the seven eyes of the LORD that range throughout the earth will rejoice when they see the chosen capstone in the hand of Zerubbabel?" (4:6-10)

Zechariah was a common name that probably meant, "Yahweh has remembered." There are some 30 different Zechariah's in the Bible, but this Zechariah was a priest who brought encouraging words to the people of Judah, who desperately needed encouragement after having survived an exile of 70 years from their blessed land.

This book is a challenge to understand since it mixes historical events with prophetic. Zechariah, is considered by Charles Ryrie, a Christian writer and theologian, to be a book about the Messiah: "Zechariah predicted more about the Messiah than any other prophet except Isaiah."

Zechariah dovetails with its neighboring book, Haggai. Haggai presented four sermons in four months and then disappeared from the scene. Two months after Haggai preached his last sermon, Zechariah began his ministry. Where Haggai spoke to the challenges of finishing the temple, which had been placed on hold, Zechariah takes us through the temple's completion (515 B.C.) and how Israel would be blessed and become a blessing through the Messiah. These are encouraging words, albeit words that were most likely misunderstood in their day but are clear in our day. Zechariah contains eight visions in its first six chapters:

Vision	Reference	Meaning
Red-horse Rider	1:7-17	God's anger against the nations
Four Horns	1:18-21	God's judgment on the nations
Surveyor with Measuring Line	Ch. 2	God's future blessing to Israel
Cleansing and Crowning of Joshua	Ch. 3	Israel's cleaning and reinstatement
Lampstand and Olive Trees	Ch. 4	Israel will be a light to nations
Flying Scroll	5:1-4	Judgment on individual Israelites
Woman in a Basket	5:5-11	Removal of Israel's national sin
Four Chariots	6:1-8	Judgment on Gentile nations

As you can see from these visions given to Zechariah, they relate to the nations that brought persecution to Judah. These nations went too far and therefore became the recipient of God's wrath. It is also clear in these visions that God remembered His promise to make Israel a great nation that would bless all people (Genesis 12:2-3; 15:5-21). These two ideas had to resonate in the hearts of the people of Judah who were exiled and wondered if their God had forgotten them.

The passage cited at the beginning of this leadership lesson is the fifth of the eight visions and portrays a gold lampstand located near two olive trees, which represent a continual source of fuel for the lamps. Zechariah was given this vision for the governor of Judah, Zerubbabel. In this passage we read of God's message of hope and good news to encourage Zerubbabel in his dark days of leadership. This vision tells the governor that he would overcome the obstacles (4:7) that would come to keep him from completing the task. It also reminded Zerubbabel that God's Spirit would work on his behalf (4:6); that he was promised that the task of completing the temple would happen on his watch (4:9); and that there would be critics who compared the size and beauty of the former temple with the one they were trying to finish (4:10).

Zerubbabel, as governor, faced incredible challenges with the task of rebuilding the temple. The good news found in Zechariah's vision no doubt helped him cope with those challenges. I'm sure that he used the hope he gained to inspire the workers in their task of finishing the temple.

As a leader, consider how good news helps you push through the barriers of leadership; but also remember that a leader who shares good news and hope is a leader who inspires others. I've known leaders who felt good news should be withheld rather than shared. I can't understand such thinking, for good news helps lift the spirit.

Thinking of good news reminds me that when I was 15, I heard the "Good News" that Christ had died for me and that I could have a broken relationship with God healed if I confessed my failures and trusted in the work of Christ through His death and resurrection. That Good News changed my life in ways I can't comprehend. Christian leader, share not only the good news of your marketplace, but share the Good News of Christ.

Reflections on Leadership:

1. There is great power in good news and hope. With your journal and pen before you, think back over your career and recall those times when good news came your way and how those words impacted your life.

2. Review the following quotes on encouragement and hope and write in your journal what you learn:

   - *"Correction does much, but encouragement does more."* Johann Wolfgang von Goethe

   - *"I consider my ability to arouse enthusiasm among men the greatest asset I possess. The way to develop the best that is in a man is by appreciation and encouragement."* Charles Schwab

#39: MALACHI

It's My Life: Isn't It?

"I the LORD do not change. So you, the descendants of Jacob, are not destroyed. Ever since the time of your ancestors you have turned away from my decrees and have not kept them. Return to me, and I will return to you," says the LORD Almighty.

"But you ask, 'How are we to return?'

"Will a mere mortal rob God? Yet you rob me.

"But you ask, 'How are we robbing you?'

"In tithes and offerings. You are under a curse—your whole nation—because you are robbing me. Bring the whole tithe into the storehouse, that there may be food in my house. <u>Test me</u> in this," says the LORD Almighty, "and see if I will not throw open the floodgates of heaven and pour out so much blessing that there will not be room enough to store it. (3:6-10)

The Scripture cited above has a somewhat sarcastic tone. We typically think sarcasm is inappropriate since it is defined as "a sharp remark or bitter taunt." The reason human sarcasm is usually wrong is because of our limited ability to understand the heart and mind of the person we are being sarcastic toward. God, on the other hand, knew the hearts and minds of the people of Judah. He knew how they had robbed Him of His tithes and offerings and made religion a lifeless practice. Therefore, God's sarcastic tone was used to make the point that Judah was clueless about what they had done toward their Creator.

Although Judah robbed God and deserved judgment, God again expressed His grace in the phrase, "Test me" and see how I'll bless you if you are obedient. Frankly, if I were God (aren't we glad I'm not?), I would not have shown such patience with Judah. The Old Testament's Minor Prophets tell Judah's story, how they repeatedly tested God through their rebellion.

God's same spirit of patience and forgiveness is repeated in the New Testament through the redemptive work of Christ and His invitation to "abide" in Him (John 15:1-8).

As you read the above passage from Malachi chapter 3, you may have noticed an attitude that is evident in our day as well—a mindset of disobedience and hubris toward God (3:7: "*Ever since the time of your ancestors you have turned away from my decrees and have not kept them*"). Such an attitude begs the question: "Whose life are you living?" This question is one that everyone must address, but leaders especially need to grapple with it in order to be leaders with a difference. Is your life yours to do as you wish, or does it belong to God as your Creator? If you are a believer, wasn't your life purchased with the blood of Christ?

It appears that most people haven't considered whose life they are living. Most struggle with the ultimate sin of pride—it is pride that keeps them from considering that God has a legitimate claim to their lives, yet He does and He hates it when we ignore His claim to our lives.

In the 1980s a Los Angeles metal band was formed called, Megadeth. No, I'm not a Megadeth fan, but the words of one of their songs; *Whose Life (Is It Anyways?)* expresses the rebellious mindset of our day:

> *Ooh, you're just in time*
>
> *To get inside my head*
>
> *Ooh, the war of words*
>
> *You're underneath my skin*
>
> *You hate the way I wear my clothes*
>
> *You hate my friends and where we go* ·
>
> *I see you in the shadows*

You think you know what's best for me

You hate everything you see in me

Have you looked in a mirror?

Hey, just whose life is this anyway?

You tell me how to live but who asked you anyway?

Hey, just whose life is this anyway?

Cost so much more than the price

I ain't going to pay

Note the words from one line in the song, "You think you know what's best for me." These words appear to be the thoughts of a youth toward an authority figure in their life, but it demonstrates the way we sometimes think about God's claim to our lives.

Have you ever thought, "You think you know what's best for me" in relationship to God's plans and leading in your life? I'm ashamed to admit it, but I have all too often closed my mind and heart toward God's directing. The 20th century English author, C.S. Lewis expressed this struggle with God poignantly in the following words, "It would be better that the door of my prison had never been opened than if it now bangs in my face! How hard to submit to God's will."

You might be asking, what does submitting to God have to do with leadership? Everything! Leaders, by their nature, often struggle with pride and have trouble being told what to do, even if their boss is Almighty God. Frankly, there is a pleasurable aspect of telling others what to do and living life without considering others. However, such an attitude is the antithesis of what godly leaders are called to be. Mark 10:42-45 vividly reminds us what is expected of godly leaders:

> *Jesus called them together and said, "You know that those who are regarded as rulers of the Gentiles lord it over them, and their high*

officials exercise authority over them. Not so with you. Instead, whoever wants to become great among you must be your servant, and whoever wants to be first must be slave of all. For even the Son of Man did not come to be served, but to serve, and to give his life as a ransom for many.

Reflections on Leadership:

1. Re-read the quote from C.S. Lewis from this lesson and write in your journal what Lewis meant and why it is so difficult to submit to God's will.

2. Reflect on the following quotes and write your thoughts in your journal:

    *   *"The degree of blessing enjoyed by any man will correspond exactly with the completeness of God's victory over him."* A. W. Tozer

    *   *"Give your life to God; He can do more with it than you can."* D. L. Moody

#40: MATTHEW

Leadership is a Lonely Place

Then Jesus went with His disciples to a place called Gethsemane, and He said to them, "Sit here while I go over there and pray." He took Peter and the two sons of Zebedee along with Him, and <u>He began to be sorrowful and troubled</u>. Then He said to them, "<u>My soul is overwhelmed with sorrow to the point of death</u>. Stay here and keep watch with Me."

Going a little farther, He fell with His face to the ground and prayed, "My Father, if it is possible, may this cup be taken from Me. Yet not as I will, but as you will."

Then He returned to His disciples and found them sleeping, "<u>Could you men not keep watch with me for one hour?</u>" He asked Peter. "Watch and pray so that you will not fall into temptation. The spirit is willing, but the flesh is weak."

He went away a second time and prayed, "My Father, if it is not possible for this cup to be taken away unless I drink it, may your will be done."

When He came back, <u>He again found them sleeping, because their eyes were heavy</u>. So He left them and went away once more and prayed the third time, saying the same thing.

Then he returned to the disciples and said to them, "<u>Are you still sleeping and resting</u>? Look, the hour has come, and the Son of Man is delivered into the hands of sinners. Rise! Let us go! Here comes My betrayer!" (26:36-46)

It can be argued that Jesus Christ was the greatest leader with the greatest assignment in history. Imagine leaving heaven knowing that your life would be one of material insignificance, you would be misunderstood by those around you and your mission was to die an unimaginably painful death for people who didn't care. And you think your leadership assignment is a tough one! Well, think again after considering Christ's assignment.

Gethsemane is the location of Christ's greatest time of temptation as He faced His imminent death. He fully understood the cost of His leadership role and wanted His closest earthly friends to support Him at this incredible time of conflict. There is deep irony in the meaning of Gethsemane, for it means "an oil press," and indeed, this place was a place of pressure in the heart and mind of our Savior. He was about to face not only His death, but separation from His Father, and the burden of taking our sins upon Himself (2 Corinthains 5:21).

Can we imagine how lonely Christ felt with His friends asleep and His Heavenly Father about to forsake Him? Three times Christ asked His inner circle of friends (Peter, James and John) to encourage Him through their "watch" and "prayer." To watch with someone means to just be there in their time of need, and prayer is seen here as a great source of encouragement and strength to the Son of God. We should learn from this scene how important it is to simply be present with those in need and the power of our prayer in the lives of others.

Abraham Lincoln led our nation during its darkest hour and no doubt experienced the loneliness of leadership. Other U.S. presidents have faced challenging times, but it was during Lincoln's watch that more than 600,000 Americans died as battle casualties on our shores.

If you haven't read Doris Kearns Goodwin's masterpiece, *Team of Rivals*, you should. This book chronicles how Lincoln chose three men who ran against him for president and invited them to serve on his cabinet. Much of the book deals with the dark days of the Civil War and the interpersonal dynamics between Lincoln and his leadership team. His second inaugural address, given five weeks before he was assassinated, contains one of the most profound quotes in history. He had watched in horror the pure evil of man and how each side of the conflict begged God for His blessing for "their side to win" the conflict:

> Both read the same Bible, and pray to the same God, and each invokes His aid against the other. It may seem strange that any men

should dare to ask a just God's assistance in wringing their bread from the sweat of other men's faces; but let us judge not that we be not judged, the prayers of both could not be answered, and that of neither has been answered fully.

This remarkable quote describes the nature of the battle we face and how humans can come down on different sides of an issue, both sides citing their interpretation of the Bible and invoking God. Lincoln's leadership during this time of war makes many believe he was one of America's greatest presidents, but have we thought about this man's loneliness and what he sacrificed in his days leading this country? The following statement by Lincoln gives us a glimpse of his heart during this lonely and confusing time of leadership.

I have been driven many times to my knees by the overwhelming conviction that I had nowhere to go. My own wisdom, and that of all about me, seemed insufficient for the day.

Leadership is paradoxical, for though you are surrounded by many, you can feel very alone. There are many lonely times when leaders are contemplating a decision, are ostracized for their actions or feel that all their relationships are predicated upon what others can get from them.

Since leadership can be lonely at times, what have you done to deal with this reality? Below are thoughts that may help the next time you find yourself alone in leadership:

- View the time alone as an opportunity for reflection and introspection rather than feeling neglected or persecuted. Alone time can be some of the sweetest times in life if they are viewed from a proper perspective. Remember, our Lord asks us to abide in Him (John 15).

- Use a journal to write out the reason for your alone time, record your feelings as you go through this lonely leadership time, write Scriptures that have proven meaningful in the past or list the various sides of a decision you need to make. Your journal entries could prove to be a source of encouragement and inspiration during the next time you are alone.

Reflections on Leadership:

1. How do you currently deal with the lonely times in leadership? Is your current method of dealing with loneliness effective or might there be a better way of viewing or dealing with it? Record your reflections in your journal.

2. Read the following quotes on leadership loneliness and record your thoughts in your journal:

   • *"It is strange to be known so universally and yet to be so lonely."* Albert Einstein

   • *"Loneliness is the first thing which God's eye named, not good."* John Milton

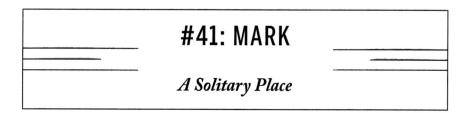

#41: MARK

A Solitary Place

The apostles gathered around Jesus and reported to Him all they had done and taught. Then, because so many people were coming and going that they did not even have a chance to eat, He said to them, "<u>Come with Me by yourselves to a quiet place and get some rest.</u>"

So they went away by themselves in a boat to <u>a solitary place</u>. But many who saw them leaving recognized them and ran on foot from all the towns and got there ahead of them. (6:30-33)

Immediately Jesus made his disciples get into the boat and go on ahead of Him to Bethsaida, while He dismissed the crowd. After leaving them, <u>He went up on a mountainside to pray</u>. (6:45)

Some background is required on Mark 6 to understand the context of Christ's instructions to His followers. This was an incredibly demanding and emotional time, with Christ having recently visited His hometown where He was viewed with contempt. He had sent His inner 12 into the countryside to minister, and He had just heard about John the Baptist's beheading. If there was ever a time for a respite, it was now. Jesus also knew they were moving into another time of ministry, so His words of wisdom to find a "solitary" location were laden with insight on the demands of ministry and work. The word "solitary" in Greek means "remote," or in this case, a place away from the fray where Christ and His disciples could find rest.

Life demands that we carve out times of silence, think time, quiet, solitude; whatever you call it, we need a place and time to "become" rather than always being busy.

Blaise Pascal (1623-1662) was one of the greatest Western Christian thinkers; he also impacted the areas of science, math and apologetics. His seminal work,

Pensées (Thoughts in French), is a collection of thoughts on how faith should address the influence of the libertines (people devoid of moral restraints) of his day. The following quote from *Pensées* is on the topic of diversion:

> I have often said that the sole cause of man's unhappiness is that he
> does not know how to stay quietly in his room.

This remarkable quote by Pascal is a truism. I have the honor of interacting with many CEOs, and one of the common themes is: focus, balance and carving out time without distraction. Today's leaders don't move at the pace of 100 years ago, let alone 10 years ago—technology has changed leadership in unimaginable ways. In a day when time is dissected into nanoseconds ($1/1,000,000,000^{th}$ of a second), leaders are driven to even more efficient ways for scheduling their day and making decisions at computer-processor speeds. Effective leadership requires both time to focus on projects, and balance in life (faith, family, fun and toil). It requires time to reflect on decisions. Even though such things are required to lead, many leaders aren't living lives of focus, balance and quiet. Why? The answer is really quite simple. We have bought into the lie that filling life with appointments, working untenable hours and doing, rather than becoming, is the best way to lead and to live life. Of course, this lie continues to be propagated in the marketplace; so few leaders are willing to strive for a better way of leading.

Living life at today's pace is our reality, and our challenge. This leadership lesson is a call for us to examine our lives to determine if they are adequately focused, in balance and providing the quiet needed to keep life in perspective.

Christ set the example of pulling away from the hectic nature of life, as is demonstrated by the Scripture passage at the beginning of this lesson. It is interesting to notice that as He and the disciples tried to pull away, the people followed them. This is the nature of leadership, for how many times have you tried to find a quiet place only to be interrupted by someone? On more than one occasion during my time as a college president, I had employees follow me into the bathroom to continue their conversation without thinking about the appropriateness of such an action!

Leaders typically work very hard. They don't count their hours on a time slip; they work until the job gets done. The typical worker in America works a 34.2-hour work week (2010 Bureau of Labor Statistics). I don't know too many leaders who only work 34.2 hours a week; they commonly work twice this amount. Leading also brings the burden of being preoccupied with work 24/7. Even when leaders have time away from the office, their mind and heart can be caught up with work through an email they read or phone call they receive. My point is, a leader's life is different and therefore requires a proactive approach to keeping it in balance.

I'm currently reading about William Wilberforce, the British abolitionist, and am taken back by his routine of study and prayer. He would spend the first hour and a half closeted for personal prayer and devotions. He often used the *Book of Common Prayer* as well as wrote his own. He viewed the first hours of the day as a preparation for what he would face, "I always find that I have the most time for business and it is best done, when I have most properly observed my private devotions."

As Biblical leaders, you know the Bible often speaks about time with the Lord, but no passage addresses this idea more poignantly than John 15. In this passage Christ reveals the need to "abide" in Him. Read the following portion from John 15 with ears to hear about the power for life that is available as we spend time with our Savior.

> *Remain in me, as I also remain in you. No branch can bear fruit by itself; it must remain in the vine. Neither can you bear fruit unless you remain in Me. (15:4)*

How much more clearly can it be said that if we remain in Christ, we will bear fruit? "What is fruit?" you may ask. It is not only a life that reflects the fruit of the Spirit, but it is also what is done in life that has lasting value, as compared to many of the things in life that have no eternal or meaningful value. John Piper provides eight practical ways to abide that offer a great foundation for moving from a hectic life to a life of purpose and power.

1. **Remind**: Prepare a way to remind yourself repeatedly of the reasons that meditating on the Scriptures is good for you (Psalm 19:7-11).

2. **Plan**: Plan a place and time when you will read the Bible and think about it each day. Put it on the calendar as an appointment.

3. **Decide**: Decide ahead of time how you will read the Bible. Also, decide how you will study the Bible.

4. **Memorize**: Memorize verses or paragraphs for this extra effort will provide the incredible benefit of driving the Word deep in your heart and mind.

5. **Retreat**: Take periodic retreats where you saturate yourself with the Bible.

6. **Journal**: Keep a journal and write out your thoughts as you meditate on the Scripture.

7. **Read**: The words of Jesus will abide in you more deeply and more powerfully if you give yourself to some serious reading of great books that are saturated with Scripture.

8. **Keep**: Keep Jesus before you as you read the Bible, and consciously remind yourself repeatedly that these are the words not of a dead teacher, but of the living Christ, who is as near as your own breathing and who is infinitely powerful.[3]

Let's close with a profound question. If Christ (the Son of God and God in flesh) spent time in quiet as He faced the rigors of His life, how much more do we need time to abide? As rhetorical as this question sounds, some of you reading this lesson will try to live life without abiding, and thus miss out on bearing the fruit you were designed for in life. Packing your schedule with appointments and always doing rather and becoming seems wise, but frankly, it is settling for second best.

---

3. from a January 3, 1993 message, *"If My Words Abide in You,"* by John Piper

Reflections on Leadership:

1. Do a 360-degree evaluation of your life (family, assistant, direct re-ports and board) as to how focused, balanced and reflective you are. From this input, determine if you are where you would like to be and devise a plan that will improve this vital area of your leadership life.

2. Reflect on the following quotes about being quiet and creating bal-ance in life. After you read each quote, write your thoughts in your journal.

   • *"Follow effective action with quiet reflection. From the quiet re-flection will come even more effective action."* Peter Drucker

   • *"Silence is a fence around wisdom."* German Proverb

#42: LUKE

Shrewd Business

"The master commended the dishonest manager because he had acted shrewdly. For the people of this world are more shrewd in dealing with their own kind than are the people of the light. I tell you, use worldly wealth to gain friends for yourselves, so that when it is gone, you will be welcomed into eternal dwellings.

"Whoever can be trusted with very little can also be trusted with much, and whoever is dishonest with very little will also be dishonest with much. So if you have not been trustworthy in handling worldly wealth, who will trust you with true riches? And if you have not been trustworthy with someone else's property, who will give you property of your own?"

"No servant can serve two masters. Either he will hate the one and love the other, or he will be devoted to the one and despise the other. You cannot serve both God and money." (16:8-13)

The book of Luke has two unique parables: the Rich Man and Lazarus and the shrewd Servant. I'm sure that when you read the parable of the Shrewd Servant the first time you were intrigued by the dialog between the rich man and his manager as well as Christ's comments regarding this parable.

Today, shrewd has a negative connotation, for most Christian business leaders wouldn't want to be known for their shrewd business transactions. In Luke 16:8, the word "shrewd" in the Greek language (*phronimos*) means having practical wisdom and being sensible. So our possible misunderstanding of the meaning of shrewd might keep us from getting the real point of this parable.

This unique parable opens with a rich man confronting his manager for wasting his possessions. We aren't given the details of the manager's action, but apparently they were serious enough to cause the rich man to fire him. As the manager considered his lot, he realized that he needed to do something that would endear him to his boss' debtors. He crafted a plan to discount the amount the two debtors owed for purchases of oil and wheat. The deal may have taken several forms from a unilateral lowering of what was owed, dropping or lowering the rate of interest, or to dropping the manager's commission for the sales. Many commentators believe that the deal was to simply lower what was owed, but why would the rich ruler commend the manager for his shrewd dealings? A possible better understanding of this parable is that the manager dropped his commission, possibly to the amount owed the ruler so he didn't lose any money—shrewd indeed.

Parables were often used in the New Testament to hide the meaning of the story, but here, Christ gives three applications for the parable. *"For people of the world are more shrewd (wise) in dealing with their own kind than are the people of the light"* (Luke 16:8b). Christ went on to tell his disciples that He wanted them to emulate the way the world uses resources to make friends, and the implication is that these relationships could lead to spiritual impact in their lives and reward in heaven.

1. *"So if you have not been trustworthy in handling worldly wealth, who will trust you with true riches?"* (Luke 16:11). Here Christ teaches on the difference between worldly wealth and true riches, which are spiritual and eternal. The implication is that, just as the "people of the light" are stewards of earthly resources, so Christians will use the opportunity to impact the world through their faith in Christ.

2. *"No servant can serve two masters. Either he will hate the one and love the other, or he will be devoted to the one and despise the other. You cannot serve both God and Money"* (Luke 16:13). This teaching of Christ is the most obvious: You can't serve both God and money. Earthly wealth has the potential of moving a person's heart from God as we are told it is the "root" of all kinds of evil (1 Timothy 6:10).

These teachings on using earthy resources can be compiled in the following statement: *Use resources to make friends on earth so that they may come to faith; our use of earthly wealth determines how we will steward spiritual work; and be careful that money doesn't move your heart from God.* If the people of light understood these simple concepts, we would see a dramatic shift in the way Christians use their wealth.

Several years ago I read the book *The Millionaire Next Door* by Thomas Stanley. I read this book because a big part of being a college president is fund raising, and I wanted to better understand the mindset of wealthy people who don't appear outwardly wealthy. As I read the book, a donor couple to the college came to mind. They live modestly in an average home, drive used cars and don't shop at fancy stores. What they do lavishly, is give. They demonstrate by the way they use their wealth that they understand the teachings of Christ from Luke 16. Shrewd is a good word to use for this couple, for they are wise stewards and use their wealth to advance the Kingdom of God.

We can learn about shrewd business from a dishonest manager, but more importantly, how to stewardship wealth to advance God's Kingdom. As Christian leaders, our lives should reflect a very different view of our resources and we should demonstrate this different perspective like the previously mentioned donor family. My prayer for each of us is that we take heed, for the world is watching and how we use our wealth speaks volumes as to where our heart is.

Reflections on Leadership:

1. Was there anything in this leadership lesson on the use of earthly resources that prompted you to consider how you might use your resources differently? If so, record your thoughts in your journal and make a plan how to proceed from there.

2. Read the following quotes on using worldly wealth and write your reflections in your journal.

    *   *"If a man is proud of his wealth, he should not be praised until it is known how he employs it."* Socrates

    *   *"Until you are happy with who you are, you will never be happy with what you have."* Zig Zigler

#43: JOHN

Relationships

For God so loved the world that he gave his one and only Son, that whoever believes in him shall not perish but have eternal life. For God did not send his Son into the world to condemn the world, but to save the world through him. (3:16, 17)

Jesus answered, "I am the way the truth and the life. No one comes to the Father except through me." (14:6)

I love simple, for it helps us better remember and understand. So I suggest that the Bible can be boiled down to one theme: relationship. God created mankind that we might have fellowship, but disobedience destroyed this idyllic opportunity and set mankind on a different path than God intended. However, God devised a plan to renew this broken relationship by sending His Son as a sacrifice for our sin. If we believe and place our faith in the work of Christ we have forgiveness, a renewed spirit and salvation because of Christ's death and resurrection. I first heard about this plan while attending camp at the age of 15, and it was there that I gave my life to Christ, and have enjoyed a relationship with my God for 45 years.

Simple, huh? Simple for mankind, since we couldn't do anything to repair a broken relationship with God, but complicated for God to move forward with His redemptive plan, knowing the incredible price His Son would pay.

With a pad of paper and pen in hand, create a "to do" list for the rest of your life. You might think this assignment silly, but in reality it is something we should do, or life will pass by without addressing the real priorities.

If you took the challenge to create a "to do" list for life, you probably will notice something—that most of your list has to do with relationships. This shouldn't be a surprise, for our leadership lesson started with the premise that life is about relationships.

I'm sure you have considered this scenario. You arrive at your home to discover it engulfed in flames. What would you do first as you enter your burning home? What items would you save, since you only have minutes before being overcome by smoke? I suggest that your first action would be to ensure that your family members are safe, and then you would probably look for that box of pictures or family memorabilia, or find your laptop with a hard drive filled with memories. Frankly, everything else can burn, and your life can be rebuilt, but losing family and memories is one of the most devastating events one can face.

With the premise that the Bible's main theme is relationship, let's review some passages that demonstrate this thought.

- Husbands and wives: Genesis 2:18-25; Ephesians 5:23-32

- Parents and children: Exodus 20:12; Deuteronomy 5:16; Ephesians 6:1-3

- Influence of bad relationships: 1 Corinthians 15:33; 2 Corinthians 6:14-15

- True friends enhance life: Proverbs 17:17; 27:9-10; Ecclesiastes 4:9-12

- With other Christians in a dispute: Matthew 18:13-19; Hebrews 10:24

- Relationships are made alive through our relationship with God: 1 John 3:1

- Relationships in the church: Acts 2:42-47

- Loving others demonstrates our love for God: 1 John 4:11-12

- Characteristics of godly relationships: 1 Corinthians 13:4-13; Galatians 5:22; Ephesians 4:29-32; Colossians 3:12-14

We could cite countless other Bible passages that speak about how we are to relate to one another, but we must consider the most important relationship before moving on. The Scriptures from John 3 and 16 cited at the beginning of this lesson speak to this relationship, one's relationship to God through Christ. As you read these words, I trust you remembered a time when you heard the Gospel and placed your faith in the work of Christ, and how your faith opened a relationship to God. Without the foundation of faith in Christ, all human relationships will be stunted, for one cannot understand how to relate to others until they know God. I would be remiss if I didn't ask the question: Do you know Jesus Christ as your Savior? If not, review the truth of John 3:16 and 16:6, for they give the foundation of the Gospel message that God loved the people of the world enough to provide a way to renew a broken relationship through Christ.

This book is about how we can become godly leaders, so what is the connection between leadership and relationship? I'm sure you are way ahead of me: leadership and relationship are inexorably linked, for leadership is expressed in the context of relationship. Below is a passage about leadership and relationship that demonstrates how worldly and godly leaders differ.

> *When the ten heard about this, they became indignant with James and John. Jesus called them together and said, "You know that those who are regarded as rulers of the Gentiles lord it over them, and their high officials exercise authority over them. <u>Not so with you. Instead, whoever wants to become great among you must be your servant, and whoever wants to be first must be slave of all.</u> For even the Son of Man did not come to be served, but to serve, and to give his life as a ransom for many."* (Mark 10:41-45)

Note the underlined section from our passage, for herein lies the key to godly leadership mindset: humility expressed through service. Christ is the personification of this mindset, but He calls godly leaders to this same standard.

I like much of what Jim Collins writes about leadership. In his book, *Good to Great,* he describes what he calls "Level 5 Leaders." These leaders manifest the highest level in a hierarchy of executive capabilities. According to Collins, humility is the key ingredient of Level 5 Leadership and is depicted in the following formula: humility + will = Level 5 Leadership. Sadly, in the world's mind, humble leaders and greatness are oxymoronic.

Since leadership is lived out in the context of relationship, and godly leaders are to be those with a humble, servant spirit, how are you doing in blending these ideas? Do your direct reports, board and staff view you as a humble person willing to serve them, or do they view you as hubris, and too proud to serve? If you don't know the answer to this question, it's time to perform a 365 evaluation. Yes, 365, not 360, since every day you lead you are to manifest a servant's heart, knowing your place before God and man.

Leadership whose foundation is built on humility expressed through service is a powerful force, for when leaders lead from this vantage point others love to follow, knowing the leader has their best interests at heart.

Reflections on Leadership:

1. In your journal, record your thoughts on the premise that the Bible's main theme is relationship. Do you agree or disagree?

2. Re-read Mark 10:41-45 and write in your journal how your leadership reflects the ideal of humility. If it doesn't, what are your plans to make humility and service hallmarks of your leadership?

3. Read the following quotes on relationships and write your thoughts in your journal:

   - *"Do you wish to be great? Then begin by being. Do you desire to construct a vast and lofty fabric? Think first about the foundations of humility. The higher your structure is to be, the deeper must be its foundation."* Saint Augustine

   - *"Humility and knowledge in poor clothes excel pride and ignorance in costly attire."* William Penn

   - *"Strange is our situation here upon earth. Each of us comes for a short visit, not knowing why, yet sometimes seeming to divine a purpose. From the standpoint of daily life, however, there is one thing we do know: that man is here for the sake of other men."* Albert Einstein

#44: ACTS

Decisions, Decisions, Decisions

The apostles and elders met to consider this question. After much discussion, Peter got up and addressed them: "Brothers, you know that some time ago God made a choice among you that the Gentiles might hear from my lips the message of the gospel and believe. God, who knows the heart, showed that He accepted them by giving the Holy Spirit to them, just as He did to us. He made no distinction between us and them, for He purified their hearts by faith. Now then, why do you try to test God by putting on the necks of the Gentiles a yoke that neither we nor our fathers have been able to bear. No! We believe it is through the grace of our Lord Jesus that we are saved, just as they are." (15:6-11)

"It is my judgment, therefore, that we should not make it difficult for the Gentiles who are turning to God. Instead we should write to them, telling them to abstain from food polluted by idols, from sexual immorality, from the meat of strangled animals and from blood." (15:19-20)

In Acts 15, we have the details as to how early Church leaders made a decision on an issue that could have split the church in two. There was a developing rift over what would be expected of Gentiles as they joined the Church. The Jews, who felt they were God's chosen people (since they were, but had rejected God's favor: Romans 3:1-20), wanted these "new" Gentile believers to uphold the same standards that were part of being a good Jew (e.g. circumcision and dietary laws). The conflict became so heated that a contingent was sent to consult with church leaders in Jerusalem. I can only envision the heated exchanges since each leader brought their background and passion to the debate. So, let's take a look at how these first-century leaders resolved the conflict and were able to maintain unity in a very volatile situation.

Below are bullet points that outline what we know about this conflict and its resolution from Acts 15:

- There was a sharp dispute over the issue of what would be required when Gentiles joined the Church, so Paul and Barnabas were appointed to go and talk with the apostles and elders in Jerusalem. (15:2, 3)

- Paul and Barnabas were welcomed when they arrived at Jerusalem, which showed a sense of community in the early Church. (15:4)

- Some of the believers who belonged to the Pharisees argued that Gentile believers needed to be circumcised. (15:5)

- The apostles and elders met to consider the question at hand. (15:6)

- Peter addressed the group and shared God's design that Gentiles would be given the opportunity to hear and respond to the Gospel. (15:7)

- The assembly listened to Paul and Barnabas share how the Gentiles had responded to the Gospel. (15:12)

- The apostles, elders and the Church agreed with the decision that James proposed and then sent witnesses with Paul and Barnabas to ensure the decision was correctly communicated and administered. (15:22)

I'd like to suggest the following ideas gleaned from the study of this passage, but please add your own thoughts after you carefully read and study this remarkable passage about decision making.

- Conflict happens: I'm amazed at how many Christians think conflict won't or shouldn't happen. Our acknowledgement of our sin nature, plus our own experience should provide enough proof that conflict occurs—and all too often. Your leadership will have conflict, so you need to learn to deal with conflict from a Biblical vantage point rather than from merely a human understanding.

- Some folks love conflict: I know you can't imagine this, but there are those who relish starting or fanning conflict. There were two groups that fanned conflict in this passage: teachers from Judea and certain

Pharisees in Jerusalem. Note that both of these groups were from "outside" the Church rather than "insiders." As quickly as possible, identify those individuals causing the conflict. They must be confronted and appropriate steps must be taken to refute their comments. We see these early Church leaders proactively addressing this conflict, rather than running from it and allowing it to do more damage to unity.

- <u>Conflict is often emotionally charged</u>: In Acts 15, the conflict was an ethic/religious conflict—sound similar to headlines of our day? The Jews believed that since they were God's chosen people, they knew the mind of God for the new Gentile believers. As you can imagine, this conflict had the potential to destroy the fledgling Church.

- <u>Leadership is critical in addressing any conflict</u>: Apparently, there were wise leaders in the Church at Antioch, for they pushed to have Paul and Barnabas go to Jerusalem to confer with the recognized leaders of the Church. We also see leadership evident in the way the apostles and elders conferred over the issue and listened to all sides before James shared the consensus. I can't tell you how many leaders I've known during my career who were conflict-averse. They used various strategies to avoid facing conflict, none of which work: blaming others for the problem asking others to address the problem, or allowing the "elephant in the room" to be an invited guest at meetings.

- <u>Communication and accountability need to accompany the decision</u>: Note that after James shared the decision, careful steps were taken to communicate the decision to the Church and accountability was set up so that the correct message would be shared when Paul and Barnabas reached Antioch. All too often, the correct decision is made, but it fails to be communicated to those most impacted by the decision, or poor accountability measures are put in place to help implement the decision. Remember how crucial decision making is to your leadership success. Make this passage from Acts a template for your decision making since it provides a wonderful insight into Biblical decision making.

Reflections on Leadership:

1. Obtain a copy of Garry Friesen's book, *Decision Making and the Will of God*. During your reading, mark the book up, because it is filled with specific illustrations of Biblical decision making. Use your journal to record what you are learning about decision making and note how your current way of decision making differs from what you are learning from this study.

2. Recall some of the biggest decisions you have made in your life and career. Evaluate in your journal how you made these decisions and how they aligned with what Scripture teaches about decision making. Next time you have a big decision, use your journal as a tool to help you think through the decision, and then evaluate the decision-making process.

3. Review the following quotes about making decisions and record your reflections in your journal:

   • *"It's not hard to make decisions when you know what your values are."* Roy Disney

   • *"Be willing to make decisions. That is the most important quality in a good leader. Don't fall victim to what I call the 'ready-aim-aim-aim-aim syndrome.' You must be willing to fire."* T. Boone Pickens

#45: ROMANS

The Gift of Leadership

Therefore, I urge you, brothers, in view of God's mercy, to offer your bodies as living sacrifices holy and pleasing to God—this is your spiritual act of worship. Do not conform any longer to the pattern of this world, but be transformed by the renewing of your mind. Then you will be able to test and approve what God's will is—his good, pleasing and perfect will.

For by the grace given me I say to every one of you: Do not think of yourself more highly than you ought, but rather think of yourself with sober judgment, in accordance with the measure of faith God has given you. Just as each of us has one body with many members, and these members do not all have the same function, so in Christ we, who are many, form one body, and each member belongs to all the others. We have different gifts, according to the grace given us. If a man's gift is prophesying, let him use it in proportion to his faith. If it is serving, let him serve; if it is teaching, let him teach; if it is encouraging, let him encourage; if it is contributing to the needs of others, let him give generously; if it is leadership, let him govern diligently; if it is showing mercy, let him do it cheerfully. (12:1-8)

Lord Montgomery (Bernard Law Montgomery: 1887-1976) was a British Army officer who commanded the British forces to victory in Tunisia and was given responsibility to plan the British invasion of D-Day on the shores of Normandy. He is credited with outlining seven leadership characteristics for a leader in war:

1. He should be able to sit back and avoid getting immersed in detail.

2. He must not be petty.

3. He must not be pompous.

4. He must be a good picker of men.

5. He should trust those under him, and let them get on with their job without interference.

6. He must have the power of clear decision.

7. He should inspire confidence.

I'm sure that as you read Lord Montgomery's leadership traits you saw the wisdom and truth of each. Merriam-Webster defines leadership as an office or position of a leader, the capacity to lead, the act of leading. Peter Drucker, America's premiere leadership guru defines leadership as strategic in nature, "Management is doing things right; leadership is doing the right things."

I'm aware that the passage I selected for this leadership lesson is about spiritual gifting, which is to be exercised in the context of the Church; but I believe we can also learn general leadership principles from this Scripture.

The Greek word for leadership in verse 8 is "*proistamenos,*" which means to stand <u>before</u> or those who are <u>over</u>. Note the prepositions used in the definition for leadership (remember prepositions link nouns, pronouns and phrases in a sentence and typically describe position or time). That a leader relates to those they lead as a preposition shows position. There are times when leaders lead from <u>within</u> or <u>among</u> those they lead, where at other times, they lead from a position <u>ahead</u> of others. However, Biblical leadership should never lord authority <u>over</u> those they lead as demonstrated in the following verses:

> *Jesus called them together and said, "You know that the rulers of the Gentiles lord it over them, and their high officials exercise authority over them. Not so with you. Instead, whoever wants to become great among you must be your servant, and whoever wants to be first must be your slave-just as the Son of Man did not come to be served, but to serve, and to give His life as a ransom for many.* (Matthew 20:25-28)

When He had finished washing their feet, He put on His clothes and returned to His place. "Do you understand what I have done for you?" He asked them. "You call me 'Teacher' and 'Lord,' and rightly so, for that is what I am. Now that I, your Lord and Teacher, have washed your feet, you also should wash one another's feet. I have set you an example that you should do as I have done for you. (John 13:12-15)

Be shepherds of God's flock that is under your care, serving as overseers— not because you must, but because you are willing, as God wants you to be; not greedy for money, but eager to serve; not lording it over those entrusted to you, but being examples to the flock. And when the Chief Shepherd appears, you will receive the crown of glory that will never fade away. (1 Peter 5:2-4)

Another important leadership lesson from this passage is found in the adjective, which modifies leadership in verse 8—"diligently." The Greek word used here is "*spoude,*" which means eagerness, not lazy or halfhearted. It should go without saying that Biblical leaders shouldn't be lazy, but the apostle Paul felt the need to make this point, no doubt from seeing halfhearted leadership in the church.

Having served in leadership positions for almost 4 decades, I can tell you that I've known my share of lazy leaders. It always astounded me that a leader who claimed to be a Christ-follower would demonstrate the unbiblical characteristic of laziness in their leadership. Leadership should be viewed as a sacred trust between a leader and those they lead, a God-given gift to be exercised with a stewardship mindset.

This passage from Romans 12 should serve as a vivid reminder that leadership is a gifting to those who have been given its responsibility, that leading requires an understanding of your position as a servant and not as a lord, and to lead with diligence knowing that your leadership impacts others.

Reflections on Leadership:

1. Write out each of the Bible passages mentioned in this lesson about leading without lording in your journal. Reflect upon these Scriptures and record your thoughts on how you use your authority: if it is servant or lordship oriented.

2. Read the following quotes about leadership and consider how the quotes might help you become a diligent leader:

   • *"Management is doing things right; leadership is doing the right things."* Peter Drucker

   • *"Character matters; leadership descends from character."* Rush Limbaugh

#46: 1 CORINTHIANS

It's Paradoxical:
It's not Supposed to Make Sense

For the <u>foolishness of God is wiser than man's wisdom</u>, and the weakness of God is stronger than man's strength.

Brother, think of what you were when you were called. Not many of you were wise by human standards; not many were influential; not many were of noble birth. But <u>God chose the foolish things of the world to shame the wise; God chose the weak things of the world to shame the strong</u>. (1:25-27)

<u>The man without the Spirit does not accept the things that come from the Spirit of God</u>, for they are foolishness to him, and he cannot understand them, because they are spiritually discerned. (2:14)

Do not deceive yourselves. If any one of you thinks he is wise by the standards of this age, he should become a "fool" so that he may become wise. For the wisdom of this world is foolishness in God's sight. (3:18, 19a)

When you read the cited Scriptures, did you like what you read? In essence, these passages tell us we will be misunderstood and viewed as fools by most folks in this world. Probably not what you expected when you became a Christian.

The bullet points below list the main ideas from our Scripture reading.

- God's wisdom is superior to man's.

- God chose a motley crew of folks in the world's eyes as His followers. (1:25-27)

- Those without the Spirit of God are unable to accept spiritual thinking, so they view it as foolishness. (2:14)

◇ 201 ◇

- As a Christian, you shouldn't seek to be viewed as wise by the world's standard, for God views worldly wisdom as foolishness. (3:19)

In reality, living a Christian life can be confusing and even frustrating at times. Why? Because living for Christ is counter-cultural and paradoxical (a seeming contradiction that may nonetheless be true). Does this statement help make sense of why you sometimes feel like an outsider, misunderstood by family, friends and co-workers?

When I first heard the idea that living a Christian life was paradoxical, it helped clarify some of the frustrations I had in living out my faith. Below are some of the paradoxical ideas found in the Bible.

- If you want to save your life, you must lose it.

  "For whoever wants to save his life will lose it, but whoever loses his life for Me will save it." (Luke 9:24)

- If you want to be lifted up, you must humble yourself.

  Submit yourselves, then, to God. Resist the devil, and he will flee from you. Come near to God and He will come near to you. (James 4:7-8a)

- If you want to be first, you must be a servant.

  "You know that the rulers of the Gentiles lord it over them, and their high officials exercise authority over them. Not so with you. Instead, whoever wants to become great among you must be your servant, and whoever wants to be first must be your slave—just as the Son of Man did not come to be served, but to serve, and to give His life as a ransom for many." (Matthew 20:24b-28)

- If you want to be strong, you must be weak.

  That is why, for Christ's sake, I delight in weaknesses, in insults, in hardships, in persecutions, in difficulties. For when I am weak, then I am strong. (2 Corinthians 12:10)

- If you say you love God, you cannot love the world.

Do not love the world or anything in the world. If anyone loves the world, the love of the Father is not in him. (1 John 2:15)

Since this book is about leading from a different perspective, you need to consider how paradox impacts the way you lead. With leadership in mind, take each of the paradoxical ideas listed and compare them with the "typical" way the world looks at leading.

Biblical Paradox in Leading	**Worldly Leadership**
save your life by losing it	live life with one's security paramount
elevated by being humble	humility is a sign of weakness in leadership
serving others	they should serve me, I'm the leader
weakness brings strength	showing your weakness is not acceptable
love God, not the world	since God doesn't exist, loving the world is the norm

I'm sure you see the stark contrast between the two columns, and how this contrast could cause leadership frustration. You might work in a business where showing humility and serving employees are unacceptable for executive management. Worldly leadership stands as the antithesis to Biblical leading. There will be times when you find yourself in the middle, having the desire to lead like Jesus, but being expected to lead through power plays and being too bottom-line oriented. In the quote below, the great 19th century English preacher, Charles Haddon Spurgeon warns against theologies that attempt to reconcile, by means of short-sighted human logic, every apparent Biblical inconsistency (paradox). "The more you study the Bible, the more you will be confronted with the idea of how living your faith conflicts with living in the world. So the more you are able to see paradox in faith, the better you will be able to cope with "living in the world, but not of it."

Reflections on Leadership:

1. In your journal, write your thoughts about the idea of the Christian life as paradoxical. Do you agree or disagree with this concept? Does the idea of paradox help clarify some of the frustrations you have experienced in your faith?

2. Evaluate your leadership in light of the idea of Biblical paradox. Does your leadership demonstrate characteristics like— humility, servanthood and balance in your view of the world's system versus God's Kingdom? Write your evaluation in your journal, and consider practical ways you can demonstrate paradoxical leadership in the future.

3. The following quotes deal with paradox. Review and apply to your walk of faith.

   • *"I have found the paradox, that if you love until it hurts, there can be no more hurt, only more love."* Mother Teresa

   • *"I am the wisest man alive, for I know one thing, and that is that I know nothing."* Plato, *The Republic*

#47: 2 CORINTHIANS

Handling Criticism

By the meekness and gentleness of Christ, I appeal to you—I, Paul, who am "timid" when face to face with you, but "bold" when away! I beg you that when I come I may not have to be as bold as I expect to be toward some people who think that we live by the standards of this world. <u>For though we live in the world, we do not wage war as the world does. The weapons we fight with are not the weapons of the world. On the contrary, they have divine power to demolish strongholds. We demolish arguments and every pretension that sets itself up against the knowledge of God, and we take captive every thought to make it obedient to Christ.</u> And we will be ready to punish every act of disobedience, once your obedience is complete. (10:1-6)

This passage shares the apostle Paul's frustration with those who criticized the way he confronted challenges, for some said he boldly confronted in his letters, but was timid in person. It is difficult to understand what the Apostle Paul is saying without knowing the context. You might want to read through the two books of Corinthians to better understand the challenges this new church faced under Paul's watchful eye.

Corinth is located about 50 miles southwest of Athens on an isthmus. Julius Caesar had Corinth rebuilt in 46-44 B.C., so this city was one of the most beautiful and modern in Greece. It was a bustling seaport and known for its worldly ways. In fact the Greek word *korinthiazesthai* meant, "to live like a Corinthian"—a life of drunkenness and debauchery. The Temple of Aphrodite (goddess of love) was prominently located atop the Acrocorinth overlooking Corinth. It is said that the temple had 1,000 prostitutes to spread the message of immoral living, so Corinth was a challenging place for a church. Paul's letters to the church at Corinth show the many challenges (divisions, law suits, false prophets, sexual impurity, misuse of spiritual gifting and the Lord's Table) this church faced, no doubt exacerbated, because of their location in a godless city. The title of this leadership lesson, *Handling Criticism,* is a theme understood by all leaders. Remember how folks related to you before you became a leader: You were probably liked by most, but as soon as you took a leadership role, the critics came out of the woodwork. In our day, everyone criticizes leaders and thinks they know best how to lead, but most would fail miserably if given leadership responsibility.

Some in the church at Corinth were saying that Paul's letters were bold, but when he visited, he was too timid in dealing with the problems (1 Corinthians 4:18-21; 2 Corinthians 10:10). Paul gives a reasoned response to these critics in chapters 10 and 11 by reminding them of Christ's character of "meekness" (strength to accept wrongs done toward Him with calmness) and "gentleness" (to deal with others in a gracious way). Therefore, Christ's example in dealing with others should be our model. He also explained that believers should deal with life in markedly different ways from the way the world does, and that we have access to the power of God at our disposal (2 Corinthians 3-5).

Conventional wisdom tells us to ignore critics and let the issues pass, but there are times when the critics need to be silenced, as Paul chose to do in this situation. He warned them that he was perfectly willing to be bold in person (1 Corinthians 10:6), and his calling as an apostle and pedigree gave him the authority to confront the false teachers who had wormed their way into the Corinthian church.

Your faith drives you to understand leadership and life from a different platform, so you probably noticed Paul's reminder to the church at Corinth that they were to handle life from a unique perspective (2 Corinthians 10:3-5). Christians have different "weapons" (2 Corinthians 10:4) from those of the world to face the challenges of life. Below is a partial list of the weaponry differences:

World's weapons: credentials, influence, status, position and worldly wisdom (1 Corinthians 1:21, 26; Philippians 3:4-8)

Not-of-this-world weapons: meekness, gentleness, truth, prayer and dependence on God (Ephesians 6:10-18; 1 Corinthians 2:4-5)

Christians are to think and act as people redeemed from the influences and thinking of the world. The following passages from Ephesians and James are poignant reminders of the differences and should serve as a mirror to evaluate our lives before God.

> *As for you, you were dead in your transgressions and sins, in which you used to live when you followed the ways of this world and of the ruler of the kingdom of the air, the spirit who is now at work in those who are disobedient. All of us also lived among them at one time, gratifying the cravings of our sinful nature and following its desires and thoughts. Like the rest, we were by nature objects of wrath. But because of his great love for us, God, who is rich in mercy, made us alive with Christ even when we were dead in transgressions—it is by grace you have been saved.* (Ephesians 2:1-5)

> *Such "wisdom" does not come down from heaven but is earthly, unspiritual, of the devil. For where you have envy and selfish ambition, there you find disorder and every evil practice. But the wisdom that comes from heaven is first of all pure; then peace-loving, considerate, submissive, full of mercy and good fruit, impartial and sincere.* (James 3:15-17)

Reflections on Leadership:

1. Re-read the Scripture cited at the beginning of this lesson about how Paul was criticized for handling false prophets. Now, review your time in leadership and try to remember a time when you were criticized for the way you handled a situation. In reflection, should you have handled the issue differently? If so, how?

2. Review the following quotes on dealing with criticism and record your thoughts in your journal.

   • *"Criticism may not be agreeable, but it is necessary. It fulfils the same function as pain in the human body; it calls attention to the development of an unhealthy state of things. If it is heeded in time, danger may be averted; if it is suppressed, a fatal distemper may develop."* Winston S. Churchill

   • *"The trouble with most of us is that we would rather be ruined by praise than saved by criticism."* Norman Vincent Peale

   • *"Any fool can criticize, condemn and complain and most fools do."* Benjamin Franklin

48: GALATIANS

Fruitful Leadership

The acts of the sinful nature are obvious: sexual immorality, impurity and debauchery; idolatry and witchcraft; hatred, discord, jealousy, fits of rage, selfish ambition, dissensions, factions and envy; drunkenness, orgies, and the like. I warn you, as I did before, that those who live like this will not inherit the kingdom of God.

But the fruit of the Spirit is love, joy, peace, patience, kindness, goodness, faithfulness, gentleness and self-control. Against such things there is no law. Those who belong to Christ Jesus have crucified the sinful nature with its passions and desires. <u>Since we live by the Spirit, let us keep in step with the Spirit</u>. (5:19-25)

As you read the cited passage you undoubtedly noticed the stark contrast between living a life directed by one's sinful nature verses the fruit of the Spirit. As a leader, many of those you lead demonstrate their sinful nature through outbursts of anger, creating dissentions between employees, power plays, inappropriate language and immorality. Without Christ, such living is the norm, so why are we surprised when we see people living out their natural proclivity?

One of my favorite books is by Dean Merrill, *Sinners in the Hands of an Angry Church*. The title is its premise, that the church is angry with worldly people for living godless lives. Some may say, well, the world lives with no care for God, so why shouldn't Christians be angry? As a leader with the heart of God, I assume your reaction is just the opposite, that you are thankful for God's grace and patience with you during the time you lived a godless life (Ephesians 2:3-5). I'm not concerned about "sinners sinning" but very interested in how Christians live their lives before a watching and needy world.

After the 1992 election, Paul Cain wrote an article for *Charisma* magazine called *"Bill Clinton, God's Man?"* Below are some of Cain's reflections from the article on why the church has lost its impact in our culture and I think he has identified some real issues.

- The reason for much of the degeneration of morals in America is not the government's fault, but the church's for complaining instead of praying, fearing instead of believing. When the church stops complaining about the government and starts repenting of her own sin, the Lord will begin to move in spite of the most resistant government leaders.

- Many who appear to be on the right side of the moral issues have . . . a combination of unrighteous judgment, spiritual pride and a spirit of control that will not tolerate differences in others.

- We must not continue to worship at the feet of political movements, trying to get the government to do the church's job . . . It is not the call of the church to legislate righteousness, but to demonstrate it, and to preach it from the platform that God has ordained.

Somehow, we have bought the lie that it is our government, schools, media or legal decisions that turn the heart of a nation toward God, but has this been the case in history? Or, have nations been moved to righteousness by God's Spirit and God's people?

What the world doesn't need is a person who lives like most, following their sinful nature; but the world does need the church to live authentic faith as expressed by the "fruit" of the Spirit. Can you imagine the power of a movement of people who live lives of love, joy, peace, patience, kindness, goodness, faithfulness, gentleness and self-control?

Notice that it is the "fruit of the Spirit" and that fruit is singular, which constitutes unity. Notice also that this fruit can only be manifested through the Spirit of God, not through human effort. A theme we have discussed often through our leadership lessons is the idea of "abiding" in Christ. Each time I read John 15, I'm reminded that it's not about me or completing my spiritual to-do list, it's all about connecting with my Lord and gaining nourishment and power to bear fruit. Let's define each aspect of this Spirit-nurtured fruit to see how powerful a leader who bears these virtues might be in their interaction with those they lead.

The first three virtues of the fruit are habits of mind:

Love (*agapé*)—unconditional and the foundation of those who bear fruit

Joy (*chara*)—an abiding inner rejoicing that is not based on circumstances

Peace (*eirēnē*)— an inner repose and quietness, even in adversity

The second triad addresses how we relate or reach out to others:

Patience (*makrothymia*)—the quality of forbearance under provocation, entertains no thoughts of provocation

Kindness (*chrēstotēs*)—benevolence in action, such as God has shown to man through grace

Goodness (*agathōsynē*)—doing good to others even when it is not deserved

The final three virtues of the fruit help guide our conduct:

Faithfulness (*pristis*)—a faithful person

Gentleness (*prautēs*)—a person who is submissive to God's Word and who disciplines others

Self-control (*emkrateia*)—denotes self-mastery in curbing fleshly impulses

As you review the nine components of Spirit-produced fruit, you can't help but be impressed with a list that transforms every aspect of living—one's mind, motives and conduct. The only way you can be a leader who reflects fruit through your leadership and life is to connect with the source of power, Christ. Yet, it is this abiding concept that is often an illusive thing, given the hurried lives of leaders. Abiding is all about relationship through connectedness, communication and time with our Lord. If you struggle with abiding, please try one of the following ideas for carving out time to abide:

- Schedule an abiding appointment on your calendar just as you would any other appointment. Keep that commitment.

- If you don't have time now for abiding, get up or stay up 30 minutes more than your current schedule for the purpose of abiding.

- Ask someone to call or text you each day and give them the permission to ask how your abiding was that day.

- Consider scheduling an abiding retreat where you take several days away with the express purpose of abiding. My wife has permitted an annual motorcycle trip (it's amazing how much you pray while doing 70 mph on a motorcycle) for many years to have an extended time of abiding with my Lord.

- Talk with your spouse about your desire to be a person who abides. Discuss setting a place and time for the purpose of abiding. Perhaps this conversation might also cause your spouse to evaluate their abiding.

Reflections on Leadership:

1. In your journal reflect on the theme of Merrill's book. Have you been part of an angry church and expected the world to live like Christians? If you have, why did this mindset exist?

2. Reflect in your journal about those with whom you work. Do you view them negatively because of the way they think and act? Have you ever considered that they think and act the way they do because they haven't experienced the grace of God in their lives? Now, inspect your fruit as a leader and ask if you have been a leader in step with the Spirit of God.

3. Reflect on the following quotes on living out your faith and record your thoughts in your journal.

    •   *"The Christian shoemaker does his duty not by putting little crosses on the shoes, but by making good shoes, because God is interested in good craftsmanship."* Martin Luther

    •   *"How little people know who think that holiness is dull . . . When one meets the real thing, it's irresistible."* C.S. Lewis

#49: EPHESIANS

Sticks and Stones

Do not let any unwholesome talk come out of your mouths, but only what is helpful for building others up according to their needs, that it may benefit those who listen. And do not grieve the Holy Spirit of God, with whom you were sealed for the day of redemption. Get rid of all bitterness, rage and anger, brawling and slander, along with every form of malice. Be kind and compassionate to one another, forgiving each other, just as in Christ, God forgave you. Follow God's example, therefore, as dearly loved children and walk in the way of love, just as Christ loved us and gave Himself up for us as a fragrant offering and sacrifice to God. (4:29-5:2)

My life verse is found in this passage—Ephesians 5:1—so I have a special affinity with our cited Scripture. The sad thing about my life verse is that I really haven't studied it in its context (my seminary professors would be disappointed). The context of this section is how words can build up or tear down (4:29), and express our internal state be it bitterness (resentment), rage (outburst of anger), anger, slander (blasphemy) or malice (ill will) (4:31).

Words are powerful things. The idea of their power is lost in an 1862 article from *The Christian Recorder,* which expressed for the first time the rhyme "Sticks and stones will break my bones, but words will never harm me." Almost everyone has heard this children's rhyme, but it just isn't true, for words can be some of the most devastating weapons people use on one another. God's Word is replete with verses that teach us the negative power of words. The book of James provides one of the most poignant passages on words and how believers' words should be consistent with their faith.

Not many of you should presume to be teachers, my brothers, because you know that we who teach will be judged more strictly. We all stumble in many ways. If anyone is never at fault in what he says, he is a perfect man, able to keep his whole body in check.

When we put bits into the mouths of horses to make them obey us, we can turn the whole animal. Or take ships as an example. Although they are so large and are driven by strong winds, they are steered by a very small rudder wherever the pilot wants to go. Likewise the tongue is a small part of the body, but it makes great boasts. Consider what a great forest is set on fire by a small spark. The tongue also is a fire, a world of evil among the parts of the body. It corrupts the whole person, sets the whole course of his life on fire, and is itself set on fire by hell.

All kinds of animals, birds, reptiles and creatures of the sea are being tamed and have been tamed by man, but no man can tame the tongue. It is a restless evil, full of deadly poison.

With the tongue we praise our Lord and Father, and with it we curse men, who have been made in God's likeness. Out of the same mouth come praise and cursing. My brothers and sisters, this should not be. Can both fresh water and salt water flow from the same spring? My brothers, can a fig tree bear olives, or a grapevine bear figs? Neither can a salt spring produce fresh water. (James 3:1-12)

The passage reminds us that our words should be consistent with our confession. Reflect on your leadership career and consider how your words have been used in the lives of those you lead. Can you remember a time when your words tore into the heart of an employee or direct report? Now consider a time when your words elevated and inspired another in the business. I hope that this exercise helped you see the power of your words, but have you also considered that your words are the best way to see into your heart? The following Scriptures should help you reflect on these questions.

The lips of the righteous nourish many, but fools die for lack of judgment. The blessing of the LORD brings wealth, and He adds no trouble to it. (Proverbs 10:21, 22)

In everything set them an example by doing what is good. In your teaching show integrity, seriousness and soundness of speech that cannot be condemned, so that those who oppose you may be ashamed because they have nothing bad to say about us. (Titus 2:7, 8)

If anyone considers himself religious and yet does not keep a tight rein on his tongue, he deceives himself and his religion is worthless. (James 1:26)

You desire to be a Biblical leader, don't you? The most important aspect of that desire is the way you use words. This week, take special note how your words influence those you lead. Use your journal as a tool to note how you steward your words and how those around you are impacted by your words, especially your family members, for often we are the least careful with those who mean the most.

I'm sure you have noticed in the Bible how Jesus communicated to the various groups He connected with. His words were carefully chosen to encourage, admonish, teach truth or express disappointment. He also used questions, stories and personal experiences to drive His words into the listener's heart.

Since words are a critical aspect of leading, I suggest that this year you study how words are used in Scripture: both positively and negatively. Such a study can be performed with any passage you select and can help ensure that your words express the cry of King David's heart in Psalm 19:14:

May the words of my mouth and the meditation of my heart be pleasing in your sight, O LORD, my Rock and my Redeemer.

Reflections on Leadership:

1. With your journal in front of you, write on the following ideas:

    *   Write the name of a person you will invite into your life who will encourage or confront you about how you use the powerful force of words. After you identify this person sit down and ask him or her questions about how he or she perceives your use of words. This interview will serve as a baseline for your words.

    *   Take your study Bible and turn to the concordance to look up the verses listed under the topics of tongue, speech and words. What additional insight have you found from this study on the use of your words?

2. Read through the following quotes about the power of words. Write your impressions from these quotes in your journal.

    *   *"We are masters of the unsaid words, but slaves of those we let slip out."* Winston Churchill

    *   *"If you wish to know the mind of a man, listen to his words."* Johann Wolfgang von Goethe (German writer and politician)

#50: PHILIPPIANS

Watch What You Brag About

If anyone else thinks he has <u>reasons to put confidence in the flesh</u>, I have more: circumcised on the eighth day, of the people of Israel, of the tribe of Benjamin, a Hebrew of Hebrews; in regard to the law, a Pharisee, as for zeal, persecuting the church; as for legalistic righteousness, faultless.

But whatever was to my profit I now consider loss for the sake of Christ. What is more, <u>I consider everything a loss compared to the surpassing greatness of knowing Christ Jesus my Lord</u>, for whose sake I have lost all things. I consider them rubbish, that I may gain Christ and be found in Him, not having a righteousness of my own that comes from the law, but that which is through faith in Christ—the righteousness that comes from God and is by faith. I want to know Christ and the power of His resurrection and the fellowship of sharing in His suffering becoming like Him in His death, and so, somehow, to attain to the resurrection from the dead. (3:4b-11)

What's the first thing you ask someone you've just met? It's usually, "What do you do for a living?" Then, over the course of the conversation you will probably inject your level of education, where you attended school, the scope of your position, people you know and anything else that makes you look good.

Consider what these words have in common: boasting, exaggeration, hubris, narcissism and one-upmanship? They all have to do with a human problem—bragging. A huge part of the fallen nature is to brag about our accomplishments whenever we can. Then, if we don't have much to brag about, we might turn to making things up to impress others.

I worked in the world of higher education for over 30 years and this field is one that lends itself to bragging. Educational hires are almost entirely based on the college you attended and what degree(s) you earned (review 1 Corinthians 8:1 and the relationship between knowledge and boasting). Over the years, I hired primarily with education in mind because teaching at the college level requires advanced degrees, but I was more interested in personal character and competence in the classroom. Degrees earned from top schools aren't the foundation for a great faculty, especially when we read Luke 6:40, which tell us that students become like their teachers. Advanced degrees can be earned; faith and character are energized by a relationship with Christ.

Our cited Scripture demonstrates the stark differences between the worldview of this cosmos and our calling in Christ. The world is impressed by one's education, income, position, influence, associates and talents. There is nothing wrong with gaining an education, making money, having a high position, influencing others, having friends known by many or having talents. But when we become believers, each of these areas is challenged as to its motives and uses. Paul was well aware of the differences as to what he put confidence in as Saul, and his conversion on the way to Damascus turned his mindset upside down to consider his former boasts as dung.

Paul boasted about two areas of his life: one given at birth (e.g. circumcision, stock of Israel, tribe of Benjamin and a Hebrew of Hebrews). The other area was his accomplishments (e.g. becoming a Pharisee, persecuting the church and having a record of legalistic righteousness). At one time, Paul's life focused on those things that gain us points from the world's perspective, but his conversion changed every aspect of life and took him in a completely different direction than he had planned.

Consider the following questions about boasting:

- Can you relate to Paul's change from boasting about the things viewed as important by the world to those important to God?

- Does your faith help you see the difference in what we should boast about ("... *let the one who boasts, boast in the Lord.*" 2 Corinthians 10:17)?

- Do your education, skills, talents, acquaintances and position keep you from fully surrendering to God?

- Do you boast?

- Do you feel pressured to brag?

Paul's words challenge us to the very core of our faith, which calls us to boast in completely different things than the world. We will feel tremendous pressure to lock step with the world in our bragging, but here is another paradoxical aspect of Christianity (see our Leadership Lesson #46: *It's Paradoxical: It's Not Supposed to Make Sense*). Remember, a paradox is a concept that doesn't appear true at first, but upon closer examination is. The paradox is the idea that the world tells us that we need to brag to get ahead, where in fact; bragging doesn't guarantee we will get ahead. Rather, it might even be what destroys any possibilities of advancement because bragging is perceived as prideful and encourages exaggeration or lying.

As a spiritual leader, shun the pressure to brag other than in what Christ has done for you through His grace. Here is an opportunity to lead differently, not as one who is consumed with a personal agenda, but rather with what Christ wants to do through you in the lives of those you lead.

Reflections on Leadership:

1. Journal your thoughts on how you might keep from bragging about the wrong things, knowing there is constant pressure to "pound your chest" to be perceived as important as a leader.

2. Read the following quotes on bragging and write your reflections in your journal.

   • *"Nothing is more deceitful than the appearance of humility. It is often only carelessness of opinion, and sometimes an indirect boast."* Jane Austen

   • *Come now, you who say, "Today or tomorrow we will go into such and such a town and spend a year there and trade and make a profit"— yet you do not know what tomorrow will bring. What is your life? For you are a mist that appears for a little time and then vanishes. Instead you ought to say, "If the Lord wills, we will live and do this or that." As it is, you brag in your arrogance. All such boasting is evil. So whoever knows the right thing to do and fails to do it, for him it is sin. (James 4:13-17)*

#51: COLOSSIANS

Opportunities Abound

Devote yourselves to <u>prayer</u>, being <u>watchful</u> and <u>thankful</u>. And pray for us, too, that God may open a door for our message, so that we may proclaim the mystery of Christ, for which I am in chains. Pray that I may proclaim it clearly, as I should. Be wise in the way you act <u>toward</u> <u>outsiders</u>; make the most of <u>every opportunity</u>. Let your conversation be always <u>full of grace</u>, <u>seasoned with salt</u>, so that you may know how to answer everyone." (4:2-6)

In this remarkable passage Paul challenges the church at Colossae, which was located in modern day Turkey, to pray and be watchful for open doors to minister to those outside the church. Although this challenge was written to a first-century church, it is applicable to the church today.

Maybe I got the idea from the above Scripture passage, but for years I've uttered this prayer when my feet hit the floor each morning, "Father, may my life be surrendered to You this day and please open doors of opportunity to proclaim Your name." I'm not suggesting you utter this prayer each morning, but as leaders and serious followers of Christ, we are required to open our eyes to what God is doing around us. What might we see if we had spiritual eyes?

You probably noticed several underlined words in our cited passage that can help us perceive God's work at opening doors: *prayer, watchful and thankful*. The first word is *prayer*. Prayer is our number one responsibility as Christians, it is the foundation of our calling to "abide" (John 15) and it is our means of communication with our Heavenly Father. Prayer slows life down so we can listen, and it helps us prioritize life as to what is important. I love church history, and particularly stories about the reformer, Martin Luther. In 1535, his barber asked Dr. Luther about prayer. The story goes, that from this simple question Martin Luther wrote a short pamphlet on prayer called *A Simple Way to Pray*. You can download this document and read Luther's thoughts on the importance of prayer and his idea of praying through the Lord's Prayer and the 10 Commandments. He explains how important he believed prayer was in his life: "I have so much to do that I shall spend the first three hours in prayer." Today, we use the excuse that we are so busy we can't pray, but I would argue that none of us have accomplished a portion of what Luther did and, maybe, he was able to accomplish so much because he started the day in passionate, extended prayer.

The second word is *watchful*. It makes perfect sense that prayer precedes watchful, for prayer slows us down so we can hear from God and helps us be spiritually perceptive. The Greek word used for watchful means being alert or aware of our surroundings. Do we start the day in prayer and give that time the priority it deserves to engage our spiritual side, which will help us be alert or aware of what God is doing around us?

Thankful is the next word. As we perceive the doors God is opening around us, we are to have a thankful spirit for what He has done. I suggest that you try the triad of *prayer*, being *watchful* and being *thankful* and note the opportunities that come into your life.

Almost 30 years ago, I began a study of the spiritual disciplines (e.g. prayer, solitude, silence, fasting, study, etc.). A friend suggested that I upgrade my journal, which was a glorified diary, to become a place to write out my prayers. Time and again after reviewing my journal I saw how God worked in situations I was anxious about, or felt confused as to what He was trying to do through my life.

Paul follows his admonishment to prayer, be watchful and be thankful by speaking about the *Mystery of Christ* (Colossians 2:2-3). In one of the most Christocentric passages in the Bible—Colossians 1:15-19—Paul tells us the unique nature and purpose of Christ is that He is equal with God, not just another prophet, like those found in other faiths. The beauty of our faith is we have a Savior who is not only a man, but a mysterious blend of man with God (hypostatic) whose death is the only means of redemption, thus opening up a relationship with God.

Our next underlined phrase is *toward outsiders*, those outside the fellowship of the church. Many of those outside the church view us as a secret society, which is understandable, because we have our own vocabulary and a unique worldview. Since our calling and worldview often conflict with the world, we love to fellowship with believers to gain strength and encouragement. Doing this, however, makes us appear as if we are part of an exclusive club. Living a life of faith is filled with great blessings (Ephesians 1:5), but it is also not without the challenges of being misunderstood by those we are called to testify to and evangelize.

Again, my love of history helps us understand how the early church impacted its world. Today, we believe that society has never been like it is today, but in reality the fledgling church existed in a culture more challenging than ours. They thrived in a world of corrupt politics, sexual perversion and social and cultural delineation at levels we can't imagine. Yet, this church made such an impact on its world by living out an authentic faith that the world noticed. The church and its influence began to reshape thinking about slavery and the role and status of women, laid a foundation for family and influenced how the sick were cared for (as exemplified by the care they expressed during the Antonine Plague and Plague of Cyprian in the 2nd and 3rd centuries). D. James Kennedy wrote a must-read book, *What if Jesus Had Never Been Born* in which he beautifully outlines how the church impacted every aspect of life as it moved into each new country through evangelism. The first-century church turned its world upside down, so today's church could have that same impact on culture if it were more intentional in living out our faith.

Finally, notice that Paul reminds us to take advantage of the open doors God places in our path, but to do so with grace and seasoned with salt. As we interact with those in the world we need to show grace just like our God showed us before our conversion, rather than look down at the world, as if we are better than them. Remember, it is by grace that we experienced our faith and by grace we have been transformed from a hater of God to a follower. Along with grace, we are to serve as a seasoning salt. Because salt is a preservative to keep food from rotting, so too, our words and actions should preserve culture from the influence of Satan and his minions (Ephesians 2:1, 2).

Leadership by The Book is about applying one's faith as a leader. I'm sure you can extrapolate the leadership concepts from this lesson, but the takeaway is you need to be on the lookout for what God is doing around you. As a leader, you will have greater opportunities to leverage these opportunities for the kingdom because of your position of influence; therefore, live life understanding this stewardship.

Reflections on Leadership:

1. If you haven't done so already, begin using your journal as a prayer journal to write down your prayers and begin to watch for open doors. Record how God is working around you as you develop your spiritual eyes.

2. The Apostle Paul reminds us to pray for open doors. In your journal write the names of several people the Spirit of God has placed on your heart and begin to pray for them. Record what happens over the next few months in their lives.

3. Read the following quotes about prayer and write your reflections in your journal.

    *   *"God is looking for people to use, and if you can get usable, he will wear you out. The most dangerous prayer you can pray is this: 'Use me.'"* Pastor Rick Warren

    *   *"The function of prayer is not to influence God, but rather to change the nature of the one who prays."* Soren Kierkegaard

#52: 1 THESSALONIANS

Leadership and Sex

Finally, brothers, we instructed you how to live in order to please God, as in fact you are living. Now we ask you and urge you in the Lord Jesus to do this more and more. For you know what instructions we gave you by the authority of the Lord Jesus.

It is God's will that you should be sanctified: that you should avoid sexual immorality; that each of you should learn to control his own body in a way that is holy and honorable, not in passionate lust like the heathen, who do not know God; and that in this matter no one should wrong his brother or take advantage of him. The Lord will punish men for all such sins, as we have already told you and warned you. For God did not call us to be impure, but to live a holy life. (4:1-7)

I've read countless leadership books and articles, but I've never read about the importance of sexual purity. Apparently, most authors don't believe this topic is worthy of mentioning.

Mike Myatt wrote an insightful article for the January 12, 2012, issue of *Forbes* called "Businesses Don't Fail—Leaders Do." His first reason for failure is:

> **Lack of Character:** It doesn't matter what your title is, if you don't do the right things for the right reasons you will fail. Leaders who don't display character won't attract it or retain it in others. Leaders who fail to demonstrate a constancy of character won't create trust, won't engender confidence and won't create loyalty.

Character is at the core of sexual purity, for as we develop deep character it helps us resist sexual temptations. If you think about it, leaders may be tempted more in the sexual arena because they face more temptations in the limelight of leadership, and because they can let hubris creep into their lives. Below are just a few examples of leaders who apparently ignored the importance of personal character.

- Anthony Weiner, a former U.S. representative who resigned from Congress after admitting his involvement in a sexting scandal

- Jerry Sandusky, an assistant football coach at Penn State under Joe Paterno who was convicted for sexual abuse of young boys

- Mark Hurd, the former CEO at HP who lost his job because of sexual impropriety with Jodie Fisher

- Harry Stonecipher, a former CEO of Boeing who came out of retirement and vowed to have a scandal-free business only to be asked to leave two years later because of an affair with Debra Peabody

- Charles E. Phillips, the former co-president of Oracle whose eight-year affair with YaVaughnie Wilkins was exposed when she paid for $150,000 worth of billboards showing them together

- John Browne, the former BP CEO whose 40-year career ended when his homosexual lover sought to sell their story to a tabloid

- Brian Dunn, the former Best Buy CEO who resigned suddenly because of what was called an "extremely close personal relationship"

Add to this list a few people from the Bible who were derailed by their sexual appetites, and you can see how precarious this temptation is.

- David, who took Bathhheba after seeing her nakedness and had her husband murdered to cover his sin

- Solomon, who ignored his God-given wisdom and had many wives and concubines from godless nations, which impacted the way he led and his outlook on life

- Samson, who linked up with a beautiful woman from Philistine, which ended up being his undoing because of her constant inquiry into his strength

We live in a duplicitous day where we want our sexual freedom but toss leaders out when they demonstrate theirs. Which is it? We also pretend to believe that what leaders do in private doesn't impact their public lives or the decisions they make. Do you really believe that?

As followers of Christ, we believe that sex was created by God and is to be enjoyed in the context of marriage between a man and a woman. Any other sexual expression is sin. I know that such a restrictive definition of sex is viewed as puritanical, but I'm not the one saying this—it is God Almighty, the creator of sex. If one honestly considers God's design for sexual purity, one sees the wisdom, but we don't always make the best decisions because of our passions and fleshly weakness. Therefore, it is all the more important to create safety nets in our lives to keep from falling into sexual temptation.

If you really believe that personal sexual purity is important and at the crux of Biblical leadership, you may want to consider building into your life some of the following ideas:

- **Accountability.** Ecclesiastes 4:12 tells the importance of having others in your life for strength. Sexual temptation is one of the most difficult to overcome alone, but bringing another person(s) into an accountability relationship is very effective. When others know you well, they can tell when you are lying about something and can confront you. Also, knowing that someone is going to ask the tough questions is a deterrent from falling into sin.

- **Internet security.** Since the United States is the producer of 60 percent of the world's porn sites, and a large percentage of pastors say they struggle with pornography, we have a problem that isn't being addressed in the average church. The Internet changes everything by making porn easily accessible, so there is the real possibility that the reader of this lesson is struggling with pornography. The Internet is an incredible tool but a heinous evil as well, so take advantage of porn-blocking software, which will help in the battle. Pornography impacts relationships and therefore must be addressed aggressively.

- **Reflection.** James 1:22-23 tells us the Word of God is like a mirror into our soul. What is the Bible telling you about your sexual purity? The first step in addressing sin is to identify it. God's Word is a powerful tool to see into your heart. Another reflection exercise is to envision how you would feel if your spouse had an affair. This exercise can help you see the pain you would cause by sexual impurity.

- **Compromising situations.** You usually know when a situation is compromising, so why put yourself in one? Look for those areas in your life that are or might become compromising, and do whatever is necessary to build in protection. Since many leaders travel, this can be one of the most dangerous scenarios you face. I worked with a college president who wouldn't travel alone in order to ensure he was held accountable. This might sound like overkill, but wouldn't it be better to overreact than to permit your marriage to be destroyed?

- **Thoughts.** There is a Chinese proverb that says, "There is a good dog and a bad dog fighting within each of us. The one that is going to win is the one we feed the most." This thought is also found in Biblical truth in Philippians 4:8-9 where Paul tells us to fix our thoughts on what is true, honorable, right, pure, lovely, admirable, excellent and praiseworthy. Which dog do you feed regularly?

Biblical leadership is about making wise decisions, planning and understanding your business or ministry; however, at the foundation of leadership success and effectiveness are trusted relationships. Living a duplicitous life, cheating on your spouse or feeding your sexual passions with porn all lead to destruction.

If you are reading this leadership lesson and know you are found wanting in the area of sexual purity, please consider some of the ideas in this lesson, and may our gracious God give you freedom in this critical area.

Reflections on Leadership:

1. You probably haven't been asked about your sexual purity before, but this is a critical aspect of Biblical leadership. In your journal, honestly evaluate this area of your life. Ask yourself, "Do I have a problem with pornography, lustful glances and thoughts?" If you are married, do you have a fulfilling sexual life? If not, talk with your spouse about your desire to be a person of sexual purity and that he or she can help you ensure this goal.

2. Consider developing an accountability partner regarding sexual purity and other areas you intend to evaluate in your walk with the Lord.

3. Read the following quotes about sexuality and record your thoughts in your journal.

    *   *"The acts of the flesh are obvious: sexual immorality, impurity and debauchery . . . "* (Galatians 5:19)

    *   *"A girl in a bikini is like having a loaded gun on your coffee table— there's nothing wrong with them, but it's hard to stop thinking about."* Garrison Keillor

#53: 2 THESSALONIANS:

Keeping Work in Perspective

In the name of the Lord Jesus Christ, we command you, brothers and sisters, to keep away from every believer who is idle and disruptive and does not live according to the teaching you received from us. For you yourselves know how you ought to follow our example. We were not idle when we were with you, nor did we eat anyone's food without paying for it. On the contrary, we worked night and day, laboring and toiling so that we would not be a burden to any of you. We did this, not because we do not have the right to such help, but in order to offer ourselves as a model for you to imitate. For even when we were with you, we gave you this rule: "The one who is unwilling to work shall not eat."

We hear that some among you are idle and disruptive. They are not busy; they are busybodies. Such people we command and urge, in the Lord Jesus Christ, to settle down and earn the food they eat. And as for you, brothers and sisters, never tire of doing what is good. (3:6-13)

The 6th century B.C. Greek slave and storyteller Aesop wrote a fable about a grasshopper and an ant and their very different views of work. The grasshopper sang all summer long, while the ant gathered provisions for the winter. When winter came, the grasshopper asked the ant for food, but the ant refused, saying he wouldn't help the grasshopper since he didn't prepare for winter.

In 2 Thessalonians 3:10, the Apostle Paul says the same thing: *The one who is unwilling to work shall not eat.* How would such a sentiment go over in today's culture of entitlement?

Let's look at some background to this passage to better understand Paul's admonishment. In 1 Thessalonians 5:14, he makes the same statement about being idle as in our lesson's passage: *And we urge you, brothers and sisters, warn those who are idle and disruptive, encourage the disheartened, help the weak, be patient with everyone.* Apparently, some members of the church in Thessalonica weren't working because of their eschatology. Yes, eschatology made some lazy, for they believed that since the Lord was about to return, why work? This may seem funny or strange to our thinking, but it is a better reason than most use to rationalize their lack of industry.

Since our lessons are for leaders, many of you may wonder, "Why do leaders need a lesson on work? Most of us are workaholics!" You would be correct in your assessment, since most leaders I've encountered aren't lazy. In fact, most of them are what we would consider type-A personalities. (The type-A personality definition—someone who is ambitious, takes on more than he or she can handle and is a high achiever—stems from a study done in the 1950s by cardiologists Mayer Friedman and Ray Rosenman.) However, if you know you have put your leadership transmission into neutral, hopefully this lesson will challenge you to shift back into drive.

Work can be graded along a continuum with "lazy bum" at one end and "workaholic" at the other. These verses from Proverbs contrast these extremes, but hard work is clearly God's choice for life.

> *Go to the ant, you sluggard; consider its ways and be wise! It has no commander, no overseer or ruler, yet it stores its provisions in summer and gathers its food at harvest.* (6:6-8)

> *Those who work their land will have abundant food, but those who chase fantasies have no sense.* (12:11)

> *Diligent hands will rule, but laziness ends in forced labor.* (12:24)

Because I was born in 1952, some may view me as having old-fashioned ideas. (Just ask my four children!) Like so many others of my generation, I grew up believing hard work was a virtue. Through the eyes of a Midwestern worldview, those who chose to be lazy were "freeloaders." Today, however, this view of hard work is diminishing. I believe one of the reasons for this change is our understanding of human nature. From the beginning of time, people have demonstrated a propensity for laziness, thus the need for every faith and culture to address this problem through teachings and cultural and workplace expectations. Today we see a dangerous move toward accepting the negative aspects of human nature by redefining what is acceptable, be it the meaning of family, appropriate sexual expressions or acceptable work expectations. Another mindset change toward hard work has been brought on by modern technology and the ease of everyday life. These two things have exacerbated our natural tendency for laziness.

I remember a *Star Trek* episode that depicted life evolving to the point that physical bodies were no longer needed. Life consisted of a powerful brain that controlled its surroundings. As we continue down the technology road, this becomes an interesting concept, but it isn't the kind of life I desire. However, it is a fact that we use our bodies less than previous generations, thus the need to proactively build some form of exercise into our daily lives.

Today, we have greater opportunities to be physically lazy, but we can also be mentally or spiritually lazy as well. Since leadership has less to do with physical work than it does with mental activities, the way we evaluate our work is different. Biblical leadership must add to our mental acumen a spiritual component if we are to be Biblical leaders. Therefore, the following assessment might help you determine where you are on a work continuum.

Ask yourself the following:

- Are you doing those things in life (resting, reading, attending conferences, exercising, eating a healthy diet) that help you keep a mental e dge to better make decisions and have the energy that is needed to be a leader?

- Do you have balance in life—knowing that there will be times when extra hours and effort are required at work—to help you keep each aspect of life in perspective?

- Are you abiding with God through the spiritual disciples of prayer, study and reflection and seeking to apply what you learn through abiding in your leadership?

- Are you leading by setting a high standard of work ethic in your life? Do you expect those who report to you to work hard, keep the leadership sword sharp and work balance into their lives?

- Have you become lazy in your leadership? If so, what has happened (feeling exhausted, discouraged and beat up, weary of the work, fighting a natural tendency to be lazy?) to move you to this position?

Reflections on Leadership:

1. With your journal in front of you, assess your work ethic. Are you at the extremes of the work continuum (lazy or workaholic)? Whatever answer you arrive at, devise a strategy that will help move you toward a place of balance. Your plan to adjust your work must be one that takes your spiritual nature into account.

2. After reading the following quotes on work, record your thoughts in your journal.

    • *"The price of success is hard work, dedication to the job at hand, and the determination that whether we win or lose, we have applied the best of ourselves to the task at hand."* Vince Lombardi

    • *"The reason a lot of people do not recognize opportunity is because it usually goes around wearing overalls looking like hard work."* Thomas Edison

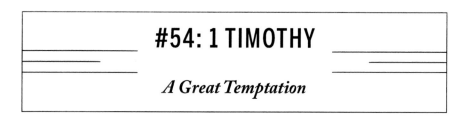

#54: 1 TIMOTHY

A Great Temptation

But godliness with contentment is great gain. For we brought nothing into the world, and we can take nothing out of it. But if we have food and clothing, we will be content with that. Those who want to get rich fall into temptation and a trap and into many foolish and harmful desires that plunge people into ruin and destruction. For the love of money is a root of all kinds of evil. Some people, eager for money, have wandered from the faith and pierced themselves with much grief.

But you, man of God, flee from all this, and pursue righteousness, godliness, faith, love, endurance and gentleness. (6:6-11)

This leadership lesson is about the love of money and material things, so we need to begin with several premises:

1. If you live in the United States, you struggle with the concept of what it means to have enough. Having had the privilege of visiting dozens of countries, I can tell you that we live in a country with unimaginable material blessings compared to almost all other countries.

2. Money isn't the main theme of our Biblical passage; rather, it's about one's mindset toward "stuff."

3. An incorrect attitude about money isn't just a rich person's problem, for someone with very little can have the wrong attitude about money.

4. Our culture is going through a metamorphosis toward money and wealth, which, in some cases, is a good thing.

5. We live in an intensely materialistic and market-driven economy that exacerbates the struggle we have with money.

An old-fashioned word best describes this leadership lesson: *avarice*. Avarice (which is also one of the seven deadly sins) is defined as an unreasonably strong desire to obtain and keep money or possessions. In 1886, the Russian author, Leo Tolstoy, wrote about avarice in his short story, *How Much Land Does a Man Need?* In the story, Pahom, a landowner, isn't happy with what he has accumulated. He's given the opportunity to buy all the land he can circumnavigate on foot in a day. He covers an amazing amount of acreage but dies as he passes the finish line. How much land does a man need? "Six feet from his head to his heels was all he needed."

Tolstoy's main character was an entrepreneur, which isn't wrong, but the combination of greed and an entrepreneurial spirit drove him literally to death. This same combination is possible in our day, but should it be part of a godly leader's thinking and behavior? I'm sure you know the answer, but Luke 16:13 reminds us that having two masters is unacceptable for a person of faith. Yet, the temptation to acquire more and more things is ever present, especially in a materialistic nation like America.

I don't know your background, but I didn't grow up in a well-to-do family. Dad enlisted in the Navy during WWII and served on a troop transport that was present in both theatres. After the war, he and my mom owned a small grocery, which opened the door to work for Continental Baking Company (Wonder Bread) for over 40 years. Our home was located in a small town in northwest Indiana and had about 1,100 square feet (two bedrooms, one bath).

My career path wasn't framed until I got a job as a dean at LeTourneau University when I was 26. That first administrative job led to a 32-year career in higher education, which allowed my family to have a lifestyle that my dad and mom could only dream about.

Why am I sharing about my career track? I believe it is a very common one for many leaders that didn't start out their careers with grandiose plans or income goals in mind. One opportunity leads to another, your income and position of power grows and you can develop a convoluted view of money. A strong faith is frankly the only thing that can keep success in its proper perspective.

How did you come to your position of leadership? Has your career advancement changed you or the way you look at things? Position and power have a way of impacting us if we don't keep faith alive and growing to keep our heart and mind in check. A passage from James 1 tells us that the Word of God is like a mirror, reflecting our true nature. Therefore, it is imperative that God's Word is part of our regular routine to keep its power of reflection for all of life.

I trust you have greed in check, but the trouble with greed is how easily it can rear its ugly head. It might happen through failing to keep your faith alive. It may arise if you get a new position that pays considerably more than the last and you extend your lifestyle to match your new income, or it might happen if you reach a position that allows you to rub shoulders with people you want to impress. Do any of these scenarios match your career path? Are you struggling to keep your faith at the forefront of your life and your position in check with reality?

The Bible and those who know us best are the greatest mirrors to reflect how we are doing with avarice. Let's never allow our leadership positions to serve as a door for greed to take hold, for this is a real possibility. In the opening Scriptural quote for this lesson, Paul poignantly reminds Timothy that craving money does a horrible thing to a person's life and can drive him or her from God.

I trust that as a leader who wants to honor your God, you don't want anything to come into your life that would drive you away from Him. Handling money is one of the most difficult temptations you will face, so make sure you do whatever you need to do to avoid its snare.

Reflections on Leadership:

1. Answer the following questions in your journal.

    *   Are you currently too interested in the things of this world (position, power, possessions)?

    *   Are you giving of your time, treasure and talent at the level appropriate to your income?

2. Read the following quotes about the influence of money upon one's life. Record in your journal any thoughts you have from reading the quotes.

    *   *"No one can serve two masters. Either you will hate the one and love the other, or you will be devoted to the one and despise the other. You cannot serve both God and money."* (Matthew 6:24)

    *   *"When it comes to money, you can't win. If you focus on making it, you're materialistic. If you try to but don't make any, you're a loser. If you make a lot and keep it, you're a miser. If you make it and spend it, you're a spendthrift. If you don't care about making it, you're unambitious. If you make a lot and still have it when you die, you're a fool--for trying to take it with you. The only way to really win with money is to hold it loosely--and be generous with it to accomplish things of value."* John Maxwell, author

#55: 2 TIMOTHY

The Ultimate MBA Curriculum

You, however, know all about my teaching, my way of life, my purpose, faith, patience, love, endurance, persecutions, sufferings—what kinds of things happened to me in Antioch, Iconium and Lystra, the persecutions I endured. Yet the Lord rescued me from all of them. In fact, everyone who wants to live a godly life in Christ Jesus will be persecuted, while evil men and impostors will go from bad to worse, deceiving and being deceived. But as for you, continue in what you have learned and have become convinced of, because you know those from whom you learned it, and how from infancy you have known the Holy Scriptures, which are able to make you wise for salvation through faith in Christ Jesus. All Scripture is God-breathed and is useful for teaching, rebuking, correcting and training in righteousness, so that the man of God may be thoroughly equipped for every good work. (3:10-17)

Obtaining an MBA is often a great means to gain access to a career in the business world. Degrees don't guarantee you have what it takes to be successful, but they do open doors. I have firsthand experience since I spent over 30 years in higher education, where a terminal degree is an entrée to teaching, but I've seen professors who had Ph.D.'s who were less than stellar teachers.

Annually, *Forbes* lists the top business schools in America. At the writing of this leadership lesson the top business schools were Stanford, Chicago, Harvard, Wharton, Northwestern, Dartmouth, Columbia, Duke, Cornell and Michigan. Most of these schools have similar courses in their curricula, such as accounting, business strategy, economics, finance, human resources, marketing management, manufacturing and production. Some of the top books used in these programs are *Freakonomics, The Winning Way, Connect the Dots* and *Positioning: The Battle for Your Mind.*

Every leader I know has prepared for their position through education (either formal or informal) and continues to grow by keeping up in their field or by expanding their expertise. These outstanding business schools and books do equip leaders for most of the issues they will encounter. They are a great foundation, but the ultimate MBA is achieved through ingesting God's manual for life, the Scriptures.

Our cited Scripture is one of the most familiar passages in the Bible. It talks about its own unique attributes, which make it the most important and useful book ever printed. Also, note from our passage that living a godly life will bring persecution, which is all the more reason to prepare for persecution through the study of God's Word.

Why is the Bible unlike all other books? Here are just a few of the unique aspects of Scripture:

- The Bible is God-breathed (Greek: *theopneustos*), or directly given by God through His inspiration to human writers. Even though it was given by God, He allowed the authors to show their personalities and styles to shine through. As you study the Bible you will be impacted by the way it constantly looks at life through God's eyes, and how its teachings are "other-worldly" compared to the writings of man.

- The Bible is unlike all other books in it addresses the greatest questions of life: Where did I come from, why am I here and what happens after this life is over? There are other philosophies that attempt to answer these basic questions, but none give hope or tell of a redemptive plan that isn't predicated on human effort. A salvation plan based on human effort will always beg the question, "Did I do enough to guarantee my salvation?"

- The Bible is unique in its message, for it was given by the One who created us and therefore knows more about mankind than anyone. Scripture has served as the basis for comfort, strength, wisdom and inspiration more than any other book in history. Every aspect of humanity has been impacted by the teachings of the Bible: education, art, music, law, business, health and relationships. I've talked with Christians who feel their faith isn't really that special, but I would vehemently disagree. A person of faith, who knows and applies Scripture has an advantage over those without the power of the Bible in their lives, for the spirit component of life has been energized adding a new perspective to every aspect of life.

Paul expands on this idea by using several words which describe its uniqueness. The Bible is the source of teaching (Greek: *didaskalia*) doctrine about God's nature and how God works in creation; the Bible is a source of reproof (Greek: *elegnos*) in that it helps us stay calibrated toward God and His will; the Bible is the source of correction (Greek: *epanorthosis*), which means to set right from an erring way; and the Bible is the source of instruction (Greek: *padeia*), which carries the idea of nurturing someone to maturity. This passage also tells us the goal of knowing God's Word is to be equipped (Greek: *artios*), a word found nowhere else in the New Testament. To be equipped means to be complete, not lacking what is needed for the task.

Do you want an MBA? Do you already have one? Whichever path you may be on, the study of God's Word and the application of it to your leadership will provide you with insight and wisdom not found in an advanced degree. Take your Bible in hand and realize the incredible resource you have to lead, not as most lead, but to lead with an infusion of God's power.

Reflections on Leadership:

1. The Apostle Paul is writing to Timothy, an elder or leader in his church. Paul tells Timothy that leadership will bring challenges. With your journal before you, what challenges have you faced in your career and how has your faith helped you deal with them?

2. Read and reflect on the following quotes about the importance of the Bible and write your thoughts in your journal.

    • *"It is impossible to rightly govern a nation without God and the Bible."* George Washington

    • *"A thorough knowledge of the Bible is worth more than a college education."* Theodore Roosevelt

#56: TITUS

A High Standard

The reason I left you in Crete was that you might straighten out what was left unfinished and appoint elders in every town, as I directed you. An elder must be blameless, the husband of but one wife, a man whose children believe and are not open to the charge of being wild and disobedient. Since an overseer is entrusted with God's work, he must be blameless—not overbearing, not quick-tempered, not given to drunkenness, not violent, not pursuing dishonest gain. Rather, he must be hospitable, one who loves what is good, who is self-controlled, upright, holy and disciplined. (1:5-8)

How important is leadership to a church, business, ministry, family and country? Some say that leadership is a linchpin, whereas others claim it isn't that important. I'm of the opinion that leadership is a linchpin, and good leaders are a challenge to find, especially when the standard of personal character is used as a criterion. The apostle Paul is also of the opinion that leadership is important, for in our cited passage he asks Titus to finish the job of appointing leaders (elders) at each church in Crete. This was a significant task for this young leader, since Crete was the fourth largest island in the Mediterranean, part of a major Roman province. Let's look at the standard used in appointing leaders in the church, for it is a high one—and one that should be used for all leaders.

The idea that leadership is crucial is confirmed by George Orwell (1903-1950, author of *Animal Farm* and *1984)*. He said, "When we trust in human oriented leadership and remove God from the landscape, dystopia is the outcome."

All too often the criteria used for leadership hinges on degrees attained, experience in a field or who you know in your network. It's not that these criteria should never be used in the selection process, but the Bible clearly states that when selecting leaders, character must be first, not as an add-on to the process. *Merriam-Webster* defines *character* as the way someone thinks, feels and behaves. So why is character often overlooked in determining if an individual should hold a leadership position? It might be because some people believe leadership skills trump character every time. This viewpoint is understandable, but skill without the rudder of character will lead to leadership decisions that reflect human wisdom and self-centeredness. Another reason is the shift to moving God and anything that smacks of faith into obscurity. As we forget the nature and character of God, we lose our sense of what character is and how well-charactered leadership benefits all those under its umbrella.

Review the list of leadership qualifications from the cited passage and note that some characteristics should *not* be part of a leader's character portfolio while others *must* be in a leader's life.

- **Blameless**. This trait is mentioned two times in this passage and means to be a person beyond reproof, or a person not open to blame or criticism.

- **Husband of but one wife**. This seems to be an almost impossible characteristic in our day; however, it is a standard that should be sought as an ideal. Remember, this is a standard for church leadership, but every leader should be evaluated on the caliber of their marriage (if applicable) for if the most intimate of relationships shows cracks in its armor, why would we think that challenges in one's marriage wouldn't show up in the leadership role?

- **Whose children believe and are not open to the charge of being wild and disobedient**. In our modern way of thinking, we probably would say, "How does the way our children behave reflect our leadership?" Yet how leaders operate in the context of their home could show how they will lead in public.

- **Not overbearing**. Recently, I was having coffee with a dear friend and our conversation moved to discuss another leader with whom we were both familiar. My friend stated that his leadership decisions reflected an arrogant mindset. I was saddened to hear this comment about another Christian leader but I knew it was true.

- **Not quick-tempered**. Everyone struggles at times with temper, often for the wrong reasons, but a leader should not be known as a person with a temper. We are all familiar with certain leaders who lead through intimidation and view their temper as a tool to be used to motivate and manipulate.

- **Not given to drunkenness**. Personal control is the issue here, for when leaders are consumed by drink or drugs, they have relinquished control to something other than themselves. In 2013, Rob Ford, Mayor of Toronto, entered the limelight for his rants while under the influence of cocaine. He made a fool of himself and doesn't deserve to continue in a leadership role, yet polls show he is still popular, which is a sad commentary for the mindset of our day.

- **Not pursuing dishonest gain**. Money and what we do with it is the main theme of New Testament parables, so making money isn't the issue; it is our motive toward it. Character is the foundation for decisions about money and how it is accumulated, for a well-charactered leader would never seek to pursue gain through dishonest means.

- **Disciplined.** Physical, intellectual, spiritual and emotional control should be a Biblical leader's lifestyle. Balance between all aspects of life and the need for spiritual understanding are key to this characteristic, for we all know those leaders who are physically fit but the more important areas of their lives are in shambles. Leadership isn't for everyone, but if you aspire to leadership, you should be held to a high standard of not only preparation and skill but also character. If you are currently in a leadership position, take character seriously with your next new hire. Illustrate the importance of character with your direct reports by setting the bar high in your own life by understanding the critical nature of leadership and seeking to live a life that is blameless in God's eyes.

Reflections on Leadership:

1. With your journal reflect upon your career and write about the criteria that were used in order for you to get each position in your career. Was character used in the selection process? How was your character judged? If character wasn't part of the selection process, why do you think it wasn't?

2. Consider the following quotes about the character of a leader and write your reflections in your journal.

   • *"Be a yardstick of quality. Some people aren't used to an environment where excellence is expected."* Steve Jobs

   • *"God grant that men of principle be our principal men."* Thomas Jefferson

#57: PHILEMON

Give Him another Chance

Therefore, although in Christ I could be bold and order you to do what you ought to do, yet I appeal to you on the basis of love. I then, as Paul—an old man and now also a prisoner of Christ Jesus—I appeal to you for my son Onesimus, who became my son while I was in chains. Formerly he was useless to you, but now he has become useful both to you and to me.

I am sending him—who is my very heart—back to you. I would have liked to keep him with me so that he could take your place in helping me while I am in chains for the gospel. But I did not want to do anything without your consent, so that any favor you do will be spontaneous and not forced. Perhaps the reason he was separated from you for a little while was that you might have him back for good—no longer as a slave, but better than a slave, as a dear brother. He is very dear to me but even dearer to you, both as a man and as a brother in the Lord.

So if you consider me a partner, welcome him as you would welcome me. If he has done you any wrong or owes you anything, charge it to me.
(1:8-18)

Paul writes Philemon, a slave owner converted through his ministry, to give a second chance to a runaway slave and thief. It is ironic that this request for grace is from a man imprisoned on account of his ministry (most commentaries believe he was imprisoned four times and spent up to six years in prison). Ironic, because Paul was imprisoned for simply expressing his faith, not like Onesimus, who had run away from his master and therefore could have been harshly disciplined. Ironic, because Paul is asking for grace, when those in authority over his life didn't show any grace in their decision to imprison him.

Ironic, that this slave came to faith in Christ and was now a brother in Christ with his owner, Philemon.

Today, we have the idea that slavery throughout history was like American slavery, but during the Roman Empire it was something quite different. A person could have been enslaved as an indentured servant (1 Corinthians 7:21 encouraged them to seek freedom), a helot who was a subjugated slave from another country through military conquest or even become a slave as part of an ancient welfare system which provided for them if they were destitute. It is also reported that Roman slaves could hold property, make a wage and get an inheritance from their owners. We don't know the reason for Onesimus' enslavement, but we know that his owner had the legal right to discipline him for running away. Sir Moses Finley, author of *The Ancient Economy,* writes that some slave owners placed riveted collars around their slaves' necks, which stated, "I have run away. Catch me and return me for a reward."

Some have expressed their disappointment that the Bible says little about abolishing slavery, but Christianity was instrumental in moving nations toward abolishing slavery as faith spread around the world. It is also clear, that if you were a believer and owned slaves you were to have a markedly different attitude toward slaves. Into this world, Galatians 3:28 expressed a radically different mindset about slaves that there was no difference between bond or free in God's view. Also, believers are to view themselves as slaves (Greek *doulos,* 1 Corinthians 7:22) toward their Heavenly Father, since our lives are redeemed (paid for) by the redemptive work of Christ.

This Biblical leadership lesson and the passage cited isn't just about slavery, but about redemption and a second chance. The apostle Paul dealt with this challenging situation with grace and wisdom. Let's look at what Paul says to convince Philemon to accept a runaway slave back without restitution. Reread the cited passage and note the following thoughts from Paul:

- Paul appeals to Philemon on the basis of love, so there was a relationship between these men because of Paul's ministry to Philemon.

- Paul reminds Philemon that he was old and imprisoned—facts that would give greater authority to his advice to accept Onesimus.

- Paul describes the radical change in Onesimus because of his new-found faith. He uses strong words about this change that Onesimus moved from being "useless to be becoming useful." Giving a second chance is predicated on the fact that the person is teachable and willing to learn, or the person has gone through a heart change, which were both apparent in Onesimus.

- Paul helps Philemon understand that when Onesimus returns he is no longer just a slave, but he is a brother in faith. What a radical view in first century Roman culture.

- Paul asks Philemon to accept Onesimus as if he were Paul. Wow, what a vote of confidence as to the change that took place in this slave.

- Finally, Paul puts his money on the line by telling Philemon that he would pay for any damages caused by Onesimus. I'm sure you noticed the uniqueness of Paul's request and the basis of the appeal to Philemon to accept Onesimus. A runaway slave was a serious infraction of Roman law, so Paul's grace approach was counter-cultural; but he had first-hand evidence that Onesimus' conversion was real and life changing. I love the idea of grace and we have an incredible story of grace in our text, but what about the grace that was extended to you in Christ? How has grace changed the way you look at others when they fail, and how can grace be incorporated into your leadership?

As I review my leadership career, there were times I "blew" it through my words, decisions and actions. Names and faces come to mind like Denny, Howard, Jim and Dean. Each of these men were my boss at some time during my career in education. Rather than putting me on the shelf and discrediting me because of my mistakes, they encouraged me and invested in me. As I reflect on these leaders, they showed grace when others might have judged me a failure for my mistakes and thrown me under the bus. I'm sure you can write down the names of those who invested in you after a mistake and gave you another chance to mature as a leader.

Reflections on Leadership:

1. In your journal reflect on those who gave you another chance after you made mistakes. How did that action of giving another chance change your life? What did those leaders do to invest in your leadership career?

2. Reflect on the following quotes about another chance or redemption and record your thoughts in your journal.

    *   *"But God demonstrates his own love for us in this: While we were yet sinners, Christ died for us."* (Romans 5:8)

    *   *"We are all trophies of God's grace, some more dramatically than others; Jesus came for the sick and not the well, for the sinner and not the righteous. He came to redeem and transform, to make all things new. May you go forth more committed than ever to nourish the souls who you touch, those tender lives who have sustained the enormous assaults of the universe."* Philip Yancey

#58: HEBREWS

So How Are They Treating You?

Through Jesus, therefore, let us continually offer to God a sacrifice of praise—the fruit of lips that confess His name. And do not forget to do good to share with others, for with such sacrifices, God is pleased.

Obey your leaders and submit to their authority. They keep watch over you as men who must give account. Obey them so that their work will be a joy, not a burden, for that would be of no advantage to you. (13:15-17)

Apparently at some point in your life you pondered becoming a leader. Did you know there is medication for that (sarcasm)? More than likely you became a leader because you demonstrated specific skills and were elevated from one position to another.

So here you are—a leader. How do you like leading? And how are people treating you?

I never aspired to become a leader but found myself serving as a president for almost half of my career in higher education. My leadership career was filled with good and poor leadership moves. At times my leading inspired others; at times it frustrated them.

This Scripture passage asks those being led to obey and submit to their leaders. Yes, those being led are called to respond to the leader a certain way, just as a leader is to respond to those they lead, especially if we are believers. Christian leaders should lead with distinction, and Christian employees should be the kind of employees every leader loves to lead. It's been said that leadership would be great if it weren't for those you lead. Of course, that's not how it works, because leadership is all about moving a group from point A to point B. As a

Biblical leader, you have to do this challenging task by leading with a servant mindset (Mark 10:42-45). Leadership is all about interacting with those you lead, so by its very nature leadership will be difficult at times. We should start with the question "Do you have what it takes to lead?" Seems like a reasonable thing to ask, and it must be answered truthfully, for if you aren't called or geared for leadership, you will hate it. If the answer is yes and you are designed to lead, you need to realize that some people will make your life miserable by the way they relate to your leadership.

I'm sure that Mary Barra—the newly appointed CEO of GM—is asking herself if leadership is her calling as she faces some of the most challenging circumstances a leader can imagine, with the huge number of recalls and deaths caused by faulty ignition switches. Brendan Eich is surely asking himself about his leadership assignment after being named CEO of Mozilla and then being pressured to resign after it was discovered he gave a donation to Prop 8 in California. Leadership isn't for wimps

The problems leaders face are the basis for many case studies aspiring business leaders study in business college. You would think that learning about the pitfalls of leadership would keep them from desiring it, but there is no lack of those who want to lead. Herein lies the problem: There are those who lead who have no business leading.

Our leadership passage provides valuable insights into what leadership is all about. Just this week, I met with a friend who is facing a season of being held accountable in regard to his leadership style and decisions. Consider the weight your leading has. Your words and decisions can lead an organization or ministry into health or destruction. You impact people's lives. Therefore, a leadership position should only be accepted after a time of prayer and seeking God's design for the appointment. I've seen too many people accept a leadership role because of the power and money it gives, but leadership is more than that; it's about serving others and seeking their best with every decision.

We love it when those we lead obey our requests and submit to our desires. Employees like this are the ones we love interacting with; they make being in charge more enjoyable. But consider how your leading makes their *following* easier. As a leader leads, so the followers follow. It can be argued that there is an eroding respect for authority today, but also can be said that this erosion is preceded by poor leadership.

Take your assignment as from God, and lead in such a way that applies the wisdom of God's Word. Seek to hear from God in your decisions, and lead from a heart of humility and servanthood. This platform of leadership often is in conflict with the world's way of leading, but that shouldn't surprise us. Don't allow your leadership to be influenced by what the world deems appropriate. You are called to a different kind of leadership.

How do you relate to those you lead? Do they obey and submit because you hold a particular position, or do they obey and submit because they know you are leading from a mindset of accountability and humility? Remember, Christ faced His critics, even though He was the Son of God, so don't believe for a minute leadership will be a walk in the park.

Reflections on Leadership:

1. Reflect on your call to leadership in your journal. How did the passion for leadership come about? How have your leadership assignments been a joy or challenge in your life?

2. Read through the following quotes about the challenges of leadership and write your thoughts in your journal.

    - *"The challenge of leadership is to be strong, but not rude; be kind, but not weak; be bold, but not bully; be thoughtful, but not lazy; be humble, but not timid; be proud, but not arrogant; have humor, but without folly."* Jim Rohn, American Entrepreneur

    - *"No man is good enough to govern another man without that other's consent."* Abraham Lincoln

#59: JAMES

Two Kinds of Wisdom

> *Who is wise and understanding among you? Let him show it by his good life, by deeds done in the humility that comes from wisdom. But if you harbor bitter envy and selfish ambition in your hearts, do not boast about it or deny the truth. Such "wisdom" does not come down from heaven but is earthly, unspiritual, of the devil. For where you have envy and selfish ambition, there you find disorder and every evil practice.*
>
> *But the wisdom that comes from heaven is first of all pure; then peace-loving, considerate, submissive, full of mercy and good fruit, impartial and sincere.* (3:13-17)

Wisdom is defined as knowledge that is gained through experiences in life, the natural ability to understand what most others cannot, knowledge of what is proper or reasonable and good sense or judgment. Synonyms are discernment, insight, perception and sagacity. It appears that wisdom is about the wise application of experiences and knowledge, which goes along with the concept of Biblical wisdom. But Biblical wisdom is also interested in how we relate to others.

The Bible is replete with verses about wisdom; in fact, the books of Job, Psalms, Proverbs, Ecclesiastes and Song of Solomon are known as Wisdom Literature. They contain wonderful nuggets of truth about living life as God designed. Below are several examples of Biblical wisdom that reveals how our character, our mindset toward God and our humility and teachability are linked to acquiring wisdom:

> *The fear of the LORD is the beginning of knowledge, but fools despise wisdom and discipline.* (Proverbs 1:7)

Do not be wise in your own eyes; fear the LORD and shun evil. (Proverbs 3:7)

A wise son heeds his father's instruction, but a mocker does not listen to rebuke. (Proverbs 13:1)

For the foolishness of God is wiser than man's wisdom, and the weakness of God is stronger than man's strength. (1 Corinthians 1:25)

The cited passage from James at the beginning provides some detail in comparing man's and God's wisdom by listing specific characteristics and its source.

Man's Wisdom
Source: Earthy, uninspired, of the devil

Characteristics: envy, selfish ambition, disorder and every evil practice

God's Wisdom
Source: Heaven

Characteristics: pure, peace-loving, considerate, submissive, full of mercy, good fruit, impartial and sincere

Note the marked difference in what happens when man's wisdom is present versus God's. Can you see how wisdom impacts the dynamics between people? Man's wisdom undermines and causes disorder, but God's wisdom seeks peace and is thoughtful of others. In the *Reflections on Leadership* part of this lesson, I ask you to journal on how man's and God's wisdom impacts the relationships around you. I'm sure you will notice the difference, but have you thought about how man's wisdom might influence your leadership style, affect how teams relate and impact how decisions are made?

Christians aren't the only folks with faith; in fact, everyone has faith in someone or something. Either you put your faith in God and seek to know His ways, or you put your faith elsewhere and accept a counterfeit truth. You can seek and apply God's wisdom, or you can accept man's wisdom, which appears true but can have a horrible impact on relationships. Since leadership is highly relational, it seems prudent always to note how one's source of wisdom can create either harmony or disorder.

Dr. Tim Irwin wrote a bestselling book about top business leaders who became derailed in life. *Derailed* is a wonderful, but tragic, book that describes how the following CEOs permitted man's wisdom to guide their leadership style and decisions.

- Bob Nardelli, former CEO of Home Depot

- Carly Fiorina, former CEO of Hewlett-Packard

- Durk Jager, former CEO of Proctor & Gamble

- Steven Heyer, former CEO of Starwood Hotels & Resorts Worldwide

- Frank Raines, former CEO of Fannie Mae

- Dick Fuld, former CEO of Lehman Brothers

Dr. Irwin's goal wasn't to point fingers but rather to provide a narrative on how a leader at the highest level can permit worldly thinking to taint his or her personality and leadership. The book outlines how each of these leaders moved through several stages toward their derailment. I can't help but believe that the root cause relates to their source of wisdom.

- **Stage One:** A Failure of Self/Other-Awareness

- **Stage Two:** Hubris: Pride Before the Fall

- **Stage Three:** Missed Early Warning Signals

- **Stage Four:** Rationalizing

- **Stage Five:** Derailment

Following are several questions I trust will cause you to think deeper about the two forms of wisdom. Give special attention to number two in which John Piper outlines how we can diligently seek and gain God's wisdom, thus keeping us from becoming derailed in our leadership.

Reflections on Leadership:

1. In your journal record business interactions you have with coworkers, direct reports, board members, customers, etc. Note in each of these relationships if the person demonstrates man's or God's wisdom and how each form of wisdom impacts your relationship with them.

2. John Piper says that wisdom needs to be desired (Proverbs 2:4), found in the Bible (Psalms 19:7) asked for (James 1:5; 1 Kings 3:11), thought of frequently (Psalms 90:12) and linked to staying close to Christ (John 15; Matthew 12:42). Reflect upon these ideas and how you seek wisdom in your life. Are you pleased with your mindset about wisdom? Do you feel you see wisdom's characteristics in your life and leadership?

3. Review the following quotes and write your thoughts as to how they allow you to be a wise leader.

    *   *"To the man who pleases him, God gives wisdom, knowledge and happiness, but to the sinner he gives the task of gathering and storing up wealth to hand it over to the one who pleases God. This too is meaningless, a chasing after the wind."* (Ecclesiastes 2:26)

    *   *"Any fool can know. The point is to understand."* Albert Einstein

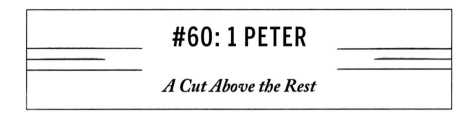

#60: 1 PETER

A Cut Above the Rest

But you are a chosen people, a royal priesthood, a holy nation, a people belonging to God, that you may declare the praises of Him who called you out of darkness into His wonderful light. (2:9)

Live such good lives among the pagans that, though they accuse you of doing wrong, they may see your good deeds and glorify God on the day He visits us. (2:12)

Always be prepared to give an answer to everyone who asks you to give the reason for the hope that you have. But do this with gentleness and respect, keeping a clear conscience, so that those who speak maliciously against your good behavior in Christ may be ashamed of their slander. (3:15-16)

However, if you suffer as a Christian, do not be ashamed, but praise God that you bear that name. (4:16)

Leadership by The Book is based on the belief that Scripture is the greatest leadership text in human history. The book of 1 Peter is a perfect example. This lesson highlights three statements, two about living "a cut above," and one about dealing with criticism even while living a righteous life.

Followers of Christ are called to the highest standard. In Philippians 4:8-9, the Apostle Paul not only defines this standard, he also challenges the church to live this way.

Finally, brothers, whatever is true, whatever is noble, whatever is right, whatever is pure, whatever is lovely, whatever is admirable—if anything is excellent or praiseworthy—think about such things. Whatever you have learned or received or heard from me, or seen in me—put it into practice.

Paul tells his readers to follow his example, which might appear like hubris but is, in fact, simply the truth because he lived his life a cut above. Just as Paul challenged the church to live unique lives, so, too, Christian leaders are called to live and lead with excellence.

In their 1982 bestseller *In Search of Excellence,* Tom Peters and Robert Waterman outlined these characteristics of excellent companies:

1. Active decision making.

2. Learn from the people served by the business.

3. Foster innovation and nurturing champions.

4. Treat employees as a source of quality.

5. Management philosophy that guides everyday practice; management showing its commitment.

6. Stay with the business that you know.

7. Some of the best companies have minimal HQ staff.

8. Autonomy in shop-floor activities plus centralized values.

After reading this book, I remember being intrigued by the soft factors (leadership characteristics, business culture, etc.) the authors identify as most important in creating an excellent business, whereas other books typically identified hard factors (numbers and statistics) as most important. While I take no issue with these qualities and can see how their presence in a company can help it thrive, I believe their list misses some of the characteristics of a leader who leads a cut above.

The idiom "a cut above" often is attributed to Shakespeare, even though he never used it in his writings. It is commonly thought to be a butcher term referring to higher quality meat cuts. Today, it refers to those who live with the highest competence, intellect or social order. Followers of Christ are called to live life a cut above.

Peter uses some unique phrases about living a life in Christ. In 1 Peter 2:9, Christians are called a royal priesthood, a chosen people and drawn from darkness to live in light, which are pretty amazing concepts when you think about it. These phrases certainly give the idea of living a cut above, so what does it mean to be a priest, someone who is chosen and living in light? It means that we are to live as representatives of God who are different from others and to proclaim truth and illuminate falsehood and sin. This is an amazing responsibility, but one the church and its members are called to in the world.

He also writes a haunting challenge to the church:

> *Live such good lives among the pagans that, though they accuse you of doing wrong, they may see your good deeds and glorify God on the day He visits us.* (1 Peter 2:12)

Can you define what it means to live a good life? The idea of a good life can only be understood when compared to the world's mindset, actions, words and motives. Read Ephesians 2:1-2 and 1 John 2:15-16. It is easy to spot worldly thinking and actions since they are incredibly self-oriented. Therefore, living a cut-above life and leading from this orientation is exactly what we hear about the mindset of Christ (Philippians 2:5-8). Note that the mind of Christ (humble and serving oriented) is contrasted with the world's mindset.

> *Do nothing out of selfish ambition or vain conceit, but in humility consider others better than yourselves. Each of you should look not only to your own interests, but also to the interest of others. Your attitude should be the same as that of Christ Jesus.* (Philippians 2:3-5)

As a cut-above leader you are really being called to be a person with position and authority who leads with humility and a servant's heart. Often position and authority convert good people into people who believe the world revolves around them. We simply don't need any more leaders who lead like that; we need leaders who are willing to lead as Christ would.

Reflections on Leadership:

1. Re-read the Scripture cited in this lesson and reflect in your journal the ideas of *"a chosen people," "a people belonging to God," "live such good lives," "always be prepared to give an answer for the hope that you have"* and *"if you suffer . . . praise God."* What do such thoughts mean to you and how do these ideas make you lead a cut above?

2. Reflect upon your past week and look at the way you have led. Did you lead as a person seeking to lead a cut above other leaders? How was your leadership better than other leaders? Did you see anything in your leadership through this exercise that concerns you?

3. Consider this Scripture and these quotes, and record your impressions in your journal.

   • *"Our chief want is someone who will inspire us to be what we know we could be."* Ralph Waldo Emerson

   • *"Example is not the main thing in influencing others. It is the only thing."* Albert Schweitzer

#61: 2 PETER

Our Raison D'être

But the day of the Lord will come like a thief. The heavens will disappear with a roar; the elements will be destroyed by fire, and the earth and everything in it will be laid bare.

Since everything will be destroyed in this way, what kind of people ought you to be? You ought to live holy and godly lives as you look forward to the day of God and speed its coming. That day will bring about the destruction of the heavens by fire, and the elements will melt in the heat. But in keeping with His promise we are looking forward to a new heaven and a new earth, the home of righteousness.

So then, dear friends, since you are looking forward to this, make every effort to be found spotless, blameless, and at peace with Him. Bear in mind that our Lord's patience means salvation, just as our dear brother Paul also wrote you, with the wisdom that God gave him. (3:10-15)

We are living in interesting times, times that cause believers to consider the Lord's return as never before. When I came to Christ more than four decades ago, there was a sense that Christ's return was imminent. This belief was reflected in books like Hal Lindsey's *The Late, Great Planet Earth*. More recently, the second coming is depicted in my friend Jerry Jenkins' bestselling *Left Behind* series.

With so much attention centered in the Middle East today, we can't help but consider we are living in the End Times. The cited passage talks about the coming judgment of this cosmos and how patient our Lord is to bring judgment so that more might receive Christ as Savior. But did you notice our calling as the Church? We are asked to live such spotless and blameless lives that we are a living witness of the power of God. Therein is the reason I titled this lesson

"Our Raison D'être"— our reason for existing. We need to be reminded that our lives are to reflect the change brought forth when we came to Christ. This change should be demonstrated in how we live and lead others. But have you ever considered your role to testify about Christ, especially as we are reminded of the impending judgment? Yes, each of us has the responsibility and joy of testifying of His grace and desire to be an instrument for evangelism. Consider how you came to Christ: Your story will be about a person who lived out his or her faith and was used by the Holy Spirit to draw you into believing faith.

As a Christian leader, have you considered how you can share your faith with those who work for you or for the company you oversee? There is the real possibility you have bifurcated your faith in your leadership role and the business world. Separating faith from part of your life can lead to frustration, but more importantly, it can keep you from living out your calling in Christ in the marketplace. This separation can also dramatically reduce the impact that your example can have on others.

You may not be the one God uses to bring your co-workers to faith, nonetheless, your faith should be reflected in your leadership. Maybe you need to seek the Lord's leading in how you might best reflect your faith through your leadership. Consider how the following companies have found ways to drive faith into the halls of business.

- Interstate Batteries: Norm Miller initiated Bible studies, missional service, philanthropy and even an evangelism program called *I Am Second*.

- Forever 21: A popular clothing retailer founded by Korean businessman Don Chang who shares his faith by printing John 3:16 on the bottom of every company bag prominently displaying faith terms in the stores.

- Tyson Foods: A small army of chaplains minister to thousands of Tyson employees.

- Hobby Lobby and Chick-fil-A: These companies decided to close on Sundays, a choice considered stupid by most business leaders. However, it was important to the company founders to openly declare their faith and give their employees time away from work.

Biblical leaders should consider not only how they are to lead with excellence and with ethical purity, but also how their faith can be shared in the marketplace. You can argue that your main role is to lead the business well. This is true, but you should also consider how you are in the role of leadership because God placed you there to bring Him glory and to share the good news of Christ.

Have you considered that everyone is an evangelist for his or her belief system? Some proselytize for hedonism, naturalism, humanism or other faiths; so why not share the incredible transformational message of the Christian faith, which has healed countless lives and is just as pertinent today as anytime in history?

Marketplace ministry is one of the most exciting and effective means of sharing Christ. I highly recommend Dr. David Miller's *God at Work: The History and Promise of the Faith at Work Movement,* which chronicles this movement and ways business leaders might share their faith. A judgment is coming, so how might our Lord use you in your leadership role to be an instrument of faith?

Reflections on Leadership:

1. Journal a time when you shared your faith in a workplace context. Can you recall such a time, if not, why not? Did you feel it was inappropriate or did you believe it was illegal? Maybe you felt unprepared to share?

2. If you agree with the premise that your life as a leader is to be a testimony for Christ, seek the Lord in how you might "up" your personal and corporate witness in the marketplace from your current faith impact. Record what you discover in your journal.

3. Review the following quotes about evangelism and think about your part in sharing Christ.

   - *"I am trying here to prevent anyone saying the really foolish thing that people often say about Him: I'm ready to accept Jesus as a great moral teacher, but I don't accept His claim to be God. That is the one thing we must not say. A man who was merely a man and said the sort of things Jesus said would not be a great moral teacher. He would either be a lunatic—on the level with the man who says he is a poached egg—or else he would be the Devil of Hell. You must make your choice. Either this man was, and is, the Son of God, or else a madman or something worse. You can shut Him up for a fool, you can spit at Him and kill Him as a demon or you can fall at His feet and call Him Lord and God, but let us not come with any patronizing nonsense about His being a great human teacher. He has not left that open to us. He did not intend to."*
   C. S. Lewis, Mere Christianity

   - *"Preach the Gospel at all times, and when necessary, use words."*
   Saint Francis of Assisi

#62: 1 JOHN

Leadership Sins

This is the message we have heard from Him and declare to you: God is light; in Him there is no darkness at all. If we claim to have fellowship with Him yet walk in the darkness, we lie and do not live by the truth. But if we walk in the light, as He is in the light, we have fellowship with one another and the blood of Jesus, His Son, purifies us from all sin.

If we claim to be without sin, we deceive ourselves and the truth is not in us. If we confess our sins, He is faithful and just and will forgive us our sins and purify us from all unrighteousness. If we claim we have not sinned, we make Him out to be a liar and the Word has no place in our lives. (1:5-10)

I Googled "leadership sins" and it was amazing how many articles and books showed up, including Jack Welch's *Six Deadly Sins of Leadership*. According to Welch, these sins are:

- **Not Giving Self-Confidence its Due.** Good leaders work relentlessly to find ways to instill self-confidence in those around them.

- **Muzzling Voice.** A know-it-all leader muzzles other voices that need to be heard.

- **Acting Phony.** A good leader can be seen grappling with tough problems, sweating the details, laughing and caring. This is what makes people respond and feel engaged with what you're saying.

- **Lacking the Guts to Differentiate.** Sprinkling resources like cheese on a pizza—a little bit everywhere—rather than understanding the need to be strategic is a mistake.

- **Fixation on Results at the Expense of Values.** Values are meaningless if leaders don't live and breathe them.

- **Skipping the Fun Part.** Celebrating makes people feel like winners and creates an atmosphere of recognition, but some leaders view celebration as unprofessional and unproductive.

Cameron Morrissey wrote a unique book, *The 7 Deadly Sins of Leadership*. He uses the classical seven deadly sins by Thomas Aquinas as his outline:

1. **Gluttony**: micromanaging or not delegating

2. **Pride**: never listening

3. **Greed**: focus too much on money

4. **Lust**: a lack of follow through

5. **Sloth**: leading without passion

6. **Envy**: being perfectionistic

7. **Wrath**: being an angry leader

I agree with both lists. Leaders need to be reminded over and over again how position and authority can encourage sinful behaviors and attitudes. Another truth about leadership sins is most leaders aren't exempt from them. So, how can we ensure these sins don't take a foothold in our lives?

First, have a relationship with God through the work of Jesus Christ. Do you know of a time when you put your faith in the work of Christ and asked for the cleansing of your sins? Without Christ you have *no* chance of overcoming the temptations of leadership.

If you have Christ, then the next most important way to avoid leadership sin is through Bible input. The following is attributed to Billy Graham:

> An Eskimo fisherman came to town every Saturday afternoon and always brought along his two dogs. One was white and the other was

black. He had taught them to fight on command. Every Saturday in the town square, people would gather and these two dogs would fight and the fisherman would take bets. On one Saturday, the black dog would win; another Saturday the white dog would win, but the fisherman always won! His friends began to ask him how he did it. He said, "I starve one and feed the other. The one I feed always wins because he is stronger.

The Bible is that which feeds our spirit and builds faith. The single most common struggle I hear from busy executives is finding time in their hectic lives to read God's Word, but there is no excuse to neglect this vital part of your life in Christ. To live life without learning to abide (John 15) is to miss out on understanding the heart of God and experiencing His power in life. Recently, I heard a CEO say, Christian leaders have an "unfair advantage" because of our relationship with Christ.

Consider the profound truth of this unfair advantage: Those without Christ are living with only a body (physical) and soul (mind and heart or emotions). They don't have the advantage of an awakened spirit, which is able to discern spiritual things. Read 1 Corinthians 2:6-16 and consider the unfair advantage you have in Christ.

With this in mind, begin to live your life as a leader seeking God's wisdom, insight and discernment. Do you really understand the wonderful wisdom you have in His Word and the discernment you have through abiding in Christ and having the mind of God? Christian leaders should demonstrate this leadership advantage, but too many of them aren't tapping into their full potential in Christ.

Next, accountability is required in order to keep leadership sins from developing. Leadership sins aren't different from other sins, but leadership has a tendency to encourage hubris, self-centeredness and materialism. One of the most important aspects of the church of Christ is to be a place of support and accountability. Life in Christ is a certain challenge in the world, so to live life and lead with someone walking with us helps keep us from believing our own

PR. Consider your career as a leader and you will probably remember a time when leadership sins grew because of a promotion, position or income. You would have stayed in that place of sin if it weren't for God's Word, His Spirit and brothers or sisters who held you accountable. Review the following scriptures, which talk about accountability, for this is a recurring theme in Scripture.

> *If your brother sins, go and show him his fault in private; if he listens to you, you have won your brother. But if he does not listen to you, take one or two more with you, so that by the mouth of two or three witnesses every fact may be confirmed. If he refuses to listen to them, tell it to the church; and if he refuses to listen even to the church, let him be to you as a Gentile and a tax collector.* (Matthew 18:15-17)

> *Brethren, even if anyone is caught in any trespass, you who are spiritual, restore such a one in a spirit of gentleness; each one looking to yourself, so that you too will not be tempted. Bear one another's burdens, and thereby fulfill the law of Christ. For if anyone thinks he is something when he is nothing, he deceives himself.* (Galatians 6:1-3)

> *. . . and let us consider how to stimulate one another to love and good deeds . . .* (Hebrews 10:24)

If you aren't abiding in the Word and prayer, start tomorrow. If you are a leader who is too proud to be held accountable, humble yourself and find a person or group where you can share the innermost parts of your life and permit them to speak the truth into your life.

Reflections on Leadership:

1. With your journal reflect on your habit of Bible intake, prayer and accountability. Be honest as to where you are with these vital aspects of your faith walk. Seek God's strength to make any changes that need to be made in order to become a person who practices spiritual disciplines.

2. Over the next month reflect how your life, heart and mind are being transformed by intentionally practicing spiritual disciplines. Record your observations in your journal. Do you feel you are becoming a leader who understands the idea of unfair advantage through the insight and wisdom you are experiencing in Christ?

3. Reflect on the following quotes about the impact of sin.

   • *"Love the sinner but hate the sin."* St. Augustine, *Opera Omnia*

   • *"Adam was but human—this explains it all. He did not want the apple for the apple's sake, he wanted it only because it was forbidden. The mistake was in not forbidding the serpent; then he would have eaten the serpent."* Mark Twain, *Pudd'nhead Wilson*

.

#63: 2 JOHN

What's Love Got to Do with It?

It has given me great joy to find some of your children walking in the truth, just as the Father commanded us. And now, dear lady, I am not writing you a new command but one we have had from the beginning. I ask that we love one another. And this is love: that we walk in obedience to His commands. As you have heard from the beginning, His command is that you walk in love. (4-6)

You may remember Tina Turner's 1984 song "What's Love Got to Do with It?" As a leader you might ask what love has to do with the CEO position, but the truth is, love is the foundation of leadership. You just need to understand the heart of God.

Review the Scripture passage from this lesson and note the number of times love is mentioned. The Greek word used here is *agape* and is best defined in 1 Corinthians 13:4-7:

Love is patient, love is kind. It does not envy, it does not boast, it is not proud. It is not rude, it is not self-seeking, it is not easily angered, it keeps no record of wrongs. Love does not delight in evil but rejoices with the truth. It always protects, always trusts, always hopes, always perseveres.

Review the list of attributes of *agape* love from this passage. Can they fit into a Biblical definition of leadership? I don't know about you, but I'd love to work for a leader whose leadership was characterized by patience, kindness and humility. I'd also like to be known as a leader who demonstrates these qualities.

This book has covered many leadership topics such as delegation, accountability, planning, dealing with critics and influencing culture, but we haven't discussed the importance of how love might make you a better leader. Read through the following questions, which are taken from the various aspects of *agape* love from a leadership context.

- Are you patient with those you lead when they make mistakes or are you overly critical and unforgiving?

- Are you known as a kind (pleasant, not harsh, generous, compassionate) person?

- Are you envious of those who have more talent or who get recognition?

- Do others see you boast about your intellect, skill and decisions?

- Do you seek your agenda and aggrandizement rather than promoting others and their accomplishments?

- Are you rude to others or caustic in your comments?

- Are you known as someone who angers easily or has outbursts that cause others to fear or mistrust you?

- Do you keep a record of wrongs others have done to you or are you able to forgive and really forget?

- Do those who work for you know your passion for doing right and hating wrong or are you known as a person who rides the fence?

- Do you protect your direct reports when others throw them under the bus?

- Are you a person who usually trusts or do you believe the worst about others?

- Are you known as a leader who is hopeful when things are difficult or are you known for worrying and being fretful?

- Do you work even harder when it is required or are you known as a leader who gives in and withdraws when challenges come?

Since leadership is done in the context of relationship, it follows suit that when a leader demonstrates unselfish love, it is the best kind of motivation rather than motivating through intimidation and fear. A *Forbes* article by Eric Jackson "The Top 8 Reasons Your Best People Are about to Quit" outlines reasons why top talent leave. The bad news is that most of the reasons relate to leadership and the good news is that they all relate to leadership. Therefore, good people will leave or stay based on how they are treated.

Loving employees as Christ loved sets a culture that people love to work in. Over and over again surveys show that employees love their work because of the environment, not simply for what they get paid. Love those you work with and insist on setting a standard of leadership that shows love.

Reflections on Leadership:

1. What areas of your leadership fail to show your love? How will you move forward to show love for those you lead? I suggest you ask your administrative assistant and direct reports how they perceive you, not just do a self-assessment.

2. The following Biblical passages are about Biblical love. Review and reflect in your journal as to the importance of love and leadership.

   • *Jesus replied: "'Love the Lord your God with all your heart and with all your soul and with all your mind.' This is the first and greatest commandment. And the second is like it: 'Love your neighbor as yourself.'"* (Matthew 22:37-39)

   • *Be completely humble and gentle; be patient, bearing with one another in love.* (Ephesians 4:2)

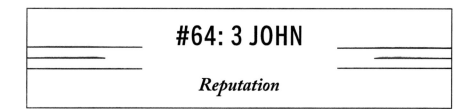

#64: 3 JOHN

Reputation

I wrote to the church, but Diotrephes, who loves to be first, will have nothing to do with us. So if I come, I will call attention to what he is doing, gossiping maliciously about us. Not satisfied with that, he refuses to welcome the brothers. He also stops those who want to do so and puts them out of the church.

Dear friend, do not imitate what is evil but what is good. Anyone who does what is good is from God. Anyone who does what is evil has not seen God. Demetrius is well spoken of by everyone—and even by the truth itself. We speak well of him, and you know that our testimony is true. (9-12)

Thomas Paine is quoted as saying, "Reputation is what men and women think of us; character is what God and angels know of us." Paine wrote *Common Sense,* which articulated the feelings of colonists prior to the Revolutionary War. His distinction between reputation and character are significant, for as believers we may have the reputation of being narrow-minded, judgmental and unforgiving. When we live out godly character it may well be misunderstood by those who don't have a spiritual perspective. All too often, however, our problem with reputation isn't one of misunderstanding, rather failure to live out our faith.

John names two men, Diotrephes and Demetrius with two very different reputations. Diotrephes was known for his pride, gossip and intimidation; Demetrius was well spoken of by everyone. Can you think of leaders who fall into these two camps of reputation?

Amber Mac recently wrote *Reputation Matters: The Top 10 Best and Worst CEOs* and listed the reputations of the 10 best and worst CEOs as determined by a survey administered by Reputation Management Consultants. The problem with this list of CEOs is it isn't based on character or skill, but what the leaders are known for primarily through social media.

Your reputation is important, but on what foundation should you build it? May I suggest on the example of the greatest leader in history, Jesus Christ. He invested in a mission for which He was willing to give His life, understood the importance of developing other leaders and multiplication and created a legacy with incredible staying power that impacted countless people. All of these goals were achieved at a level unlike any leader in history. Christ's leadership used a model some think foolish: humility and servant-minded.

John Wooden (1910-2010) was one of the most successful coaches in history having won 10 NCAA basketball championships while coaching at UCLA. He loved the Lord and believed his faith was more important than even basketball. Coach Wooden considered Christ his example for leadership and wanted his reputation to reflect his relationship with Christ as demonstrated by the following quote:

> Be more concerned with your character than your reputation,
> because your character is what you really are, while your reputation
> is merely what others think you are.

Wooden understood that *character* was the standard demonstrated in Christ's life, where *reputation* is what man thinks is important. Mankind's standard for reputation is often way below that of God's, so don't be too interested what other's think of you, for their kudos might be encouraging you to live in a way contrary to His.

The Bible was important to John Wooden. He sought to live his life by these seven statements:

1. Be true to yourself.
2. Make each day your masterpiece.
3. Help others.
4. Drink deeply from good books, especially the Bible.

5. Make friendship a fine art.

6. Build a shelter against a rainy day.

7. Pray for guidance and give thanks for your blessings each day

Remember Demetrius? I believe the reason others spoke highly of him had to do with the way he interacted with others. The Bible has much to say about how we interact with one another through the many "one another" passages:

- Accept one another: Romans 15:7

- Admonish one another: Colossians 3:16

- Bear one another's burdens: Galatians 6:2

- Build one another up: Romans 14:19

- Care for one another: 1 Corinthians 12:25

- Comfort one another: 1 Thessalonians 4:18

- Encourage one another: 1 Thessalonians 5:11

- Forgive one another: Ephesians 4:32

- Be honest with one another: Colossians 3:9

- Honor one another: Romans 12:10b

- Be kind one to another: Ephesians 4:32

- Serve one another: Galatians 5:13

If you lead with these "one anothers" in mind, others will speak highly of you. Who wouldn't love to have a leader who truly cared for them? Today we call treating others appropriately "emotional intelligence" (EI). I don't know if EI took some of its ideas from the Bible, but I do know that God is very interested in the way we treat others and how a godly character can impact our reputation and have other speak highly of us.

Reflections on Leadership:

1. What is your reputation? Record your thoughts in your journal and reflect on those things which created your reputation, either good or bad. Are you using God's standard for your reputation foundation, or do you notice you are using the world's?

2. Reflect on your answer to question one and chart how you might improve or enhance your reputation. Write your reflections in your journal.

3. Please read the following quotes about reputation and record your thoughts in your journal.

    *   *"It takes 20 years to build a reputation and five minutes to ruin it. If you think about that, you'll do things differently."* Warren Buffet

    *   *"Reputation is what men and women think of us; character is what God and angels know of us."* Thomas Paine

#65: JUDE

Word of the Day: Duplicity

These men are blemishes at your love feasts, eating with you without the slightest qualm—shepherds who feed only themselves. They are clouds without rain, blown along by the wind; autumn trees, without fruit and uprooted—twice dead. They are wild waves of the sea, foaming up their shame; wandering stars, for whom blackest darkness has been reserved forever.

Enoch, the seventh from Adam, prophesied about these men: "See, the Lord is coming with thousands upon thousands of His holy ones to judge everyone, and to convict all the ungodly of all the ungodly acts they have done in the ungodly way, and of all the harsh words ungodly sinners have spoken against Him." These men are grumblers and faultfinders, they follow their own evil desires; they boast about themselves and flatter others for their own advantage. (12-16)

Duplicity comes from a 13th century French word that means double or having two appearances. It can also mean a doubleness of speech or action, deceitful or fraudulent. In the world of faith, we call duplicity by another name: hypocrisy. Survey after survey shows that the single thing that most irritates unbelievers are Christians who say what they believe and then act very differently.

Jude calls church leaders who are hypocrites or duplicitous "shepherds who feed only themselves." Pastors or elders in the church are often referred to as shepherds since they are to lead by setting an example of Christlikeness. So, when they don't live as shepherds ought, it gives a black eye to the whole of Christianity.

Even though you probably aren't serving as a pastor, I trust you have a relationship with God through Christ as your Savior; therefore, you are also called to live a life of example. As a leader you have a greater responsibility to be an example since others look to you to set a standard. Read this sobering passage from Colossians 3:

> *Since then, you have been raised with Christ, set your hearts on things above, where Christ is seated at the right hand of God. Set your minds on things above, not on earthly things. For you died, and your life is now hidden with Christ in God. When Christ, who is your life, appears, then you also will appear with Him in glory.*

> *Put to death, therefore, whatever belongs to your earthly nature: sexual immorality, impurity, lust, evil desires and greed, which is idolatry. Because of these, the wrath of God is coming. You used to walk in these ways, in the life you once lived. But now you must also rid yourselves of all such things as these: anger, rage, malice, slander, and filthy language from your lips. Do not lie to each other since your have taken off your old self with its practices and have put on the new self, which is being renewed in knowledge in the image of its Creator . . . Therefore, as God's chosen people, holy and dearly loved, clothe yourselves in compassion, kindness, humility, gentleness, and patience. (3:1-10, 12)*

Consider the tremendous opportunity we have to be an example of a life well lived. We can be a dynamic source of light and hope when righteousness seems to be shrinking away.

Jude was disgusted with church leaders who were hypocrites. If we can have ministry leaders living in hypocrisy, so too, we can have Christian business leaders who live hypocritically. Have you made the decision to live your faith out in the marketplace or whatever leadership assignment you are in? If you haven't come to grips with this question, you might be living a duplicitous life—talking and acting one way in the church context but talking and acting like the world in the rest of your life. Far too many leaders, especially in the business arena, know the Lord but somehow haven't made a connection between living in Christ and leading in a secular environment. Why? I believe there are several reasons.

- **Fear.** You know in your heart that you should lead as Christ would, but you are fearful of the fallout if you do.

- **Ignorance.** You really want to lead like Christ, but you aren't equipped with Biblical knowledge to lead from a Biblical perspective or have never had the example of an authentic Christian business leader.

- **Carnality.** To be carnal is to have a relationship with Christ but to deny it by living as if you had no such relationship and thus negating the power of faith in your life.

If you are like me, you cringe when you hear someone speak ill about another brother or sister, for the other person's hypocrisy may well impact how people view your faith. May it never be said of us that we talk one way and live another, for what power is there in that kind of life? I want to be a leader who leads above reproach, without blemish, with no hint of duplicity.

Reflection on Leadership:

1. Have you made a conscious decision to live out your faith as a leader? If not, why? Record in your journal your thoughts on this question.

2. Is there a possibility there is duplicity in your life? Seek God through prayer and record the Spirit of God's prompting by writing a prayer about this in your journal.

3. Read the following quotes about double-mindedness and record your thoughts in your journal.

    *   *"Kids have what I call a built-in hypocrisy antenna that comes up and blocks out what you're saying when you're being a hypocrite."* Dr. Benjamin Carson

    *   *"Hypocrites in the Church? Yes, and in the lodge and at the home. Don't hunt through the Church for a hypocrite. Go home and look in the mirror. Hypocrites? Yes. See that you make the number one less."* Billy Sunday

#66: REVELATION

I Hate Lukewarm Coffee

These are the words of the Amen, the faithful and true witness, the ruler of God's creation. I know your deeds, that you are neither cold nor hot. I wish you were either one or the other! So, because you are lukewarm— neither hot nor cold—I am about to spit you out of my mouth. You say, "I am rich; I have acquired wealth and do not need a thing." But you do not realize that you are wretched, pitiful, poor, blind and naked. Those whom I love I rebuke and discipline. (3:14-17, 19)

If you spend anytime with me, you will find out that one of my great loves is strong coffee. I have lived in Phoenix for over 20 years, so I've done my share of hot summers, but there is one advantage I've discovered about our hot weather. When I leave my coffee in the car in the morning, when I get in the car that afternoon, my coffee is hotter than when I left it! Wow, hot coffee to enjoy on my drive home at 110 degrees.

As lukewarm temperature strips the flavor from a strong cup of coffee, so, too, a life lived in a lukewarm manner negates its flavor.

We usually go to Revelation to study eschatology, but chapters two and three seem somewhat disjointed from the rest of this book. Scholars tell us that this section provides a unique insight into first century churches in Asia Minor and also has an eerie similarity to the history of the church. The apostle John had a thorough understanding of the church scene in Asia Minor since he pastored the church in Ephesus, and the lukewarm Church mentioned here was located in Laodicea, a center for commerce. John lived his life as far from lukewarm as possible. He was:

- one of the first chosen by Christ

- a member of the inner circle with Peter and James

- known as the beloved disciple

- the writer of five New Testament books

- the disciple who teamed up with Peter to become the bold leaders of the fledgling church after Pentecost.

This boldness brought about persecution while he pastored in Ephesus and exile to the small mining island of Patmos (southwest of Ephesus in modern day Turkey in the Aegean Sea). So when John rebukes the Laodicean church for their being lukewarm, he is speaking from a heart of love for the cause of Christ that it not be diluted through complacency.

As a church leader who suffered for his faith, John understood the need to confront those churches and members who had moved toward lukewarmness or had lost their first love (church at Ephesus—2:4). Leaders today also must realize that living out faith will require a constant vigil to keep one's faith "hot."

Note, too, that physical comfort (v. 17) can have an impact on moving one toward a lukewarm faith. Leadership can bring material comfort, so be careful that this comfort doesn't translate into a cooling of your faith.

As a Christian writer, C. S. Lewis is best known for his masterful book, *Mere Christianity*. In it he challenges us to maintain a passion for Christ and not to allow the counterfeit pleasures of the world to dull our faith walk.

> The Christian says, "Creatures are not born with desires unless satisfaction for those desires exists. A baby feels hunger: well, there is such a thing as food. A duckling wants to swim: well, there is such a thing as water. Men feel sexual desire: well, there is such a thing as sex. If I find in myself a desire which no experience in this world can satisfy, the most probable explanation is that I was made for another world. If none of my earthly pleasures satisfy it, that does not prove that the universe is a fraud. Probably earthly pleasures were never meant to satisfy it, but only to arouse it, to suggest the real thing. If

that is so, I must take care, on the one hand, never to despise, or to be unthankful for, these earthly blessings, and on the other, never to mistake them for the something else of which they are only a kind of copy, or echo, or mirage. I must keep alive in myself the desire for my true country, which I shall not find till after death; I must never let it get snowed under or turned aside; I must make it the main object of life to press on to that country and to help others to do the same."

—C. S. Lewis, *Mere Christianity*

If you don't tolerate lukewarm employees, why would you permit this same mindset in your life or other brothers or sisters in Christ? John is a wonderful example of a church leader who lived his life with abandon. As we close this series of 66 leadership lessons from the Bible, I trust you have been challenged to live out your faith in the marketplace, to allow others into your life to hold you accountable and to use the Scriptures as your primary source of leadership wisdom.

Lead well (Romans 12:8), lead with uniqueness as Christ led and changed the world through a solitary life well lived.

Reflections on Leadership:

Review your journal entries from the last 66 chapters and write a compendium of thoughts or reflections from this book.

1. Write a plan from your reflections as to progress you have made toward becoming a Biblical leader and set resolutions for additional changes that need to be made.

2. Review the following quotes about living life to its fullest and note your reflections in your journal.

   • *"The time you spend alone with God will transform your character and increase your devotion. Then your integrity and godly behavior in an unbelieving world will make others long to know the Lord."* Charles Stanley

   • *"It was becoming clearer and clearer that if I wanted to come to the end of my life and not say, "I've wasted it!" then I would need to press all the way in, and all the way up, to the ultimate purpose of God and join him in it. If my life was to have a single, all-satisfying, unifying passion, it would have to be God's passion."* John Piper, pastor and author

A Final Thought

You've just finished reading 66 bite-sized leadership lessons. How did it taste to your leadership palate? If you recall, I suggested in the introduction of this book that one of my goals was to help you see the Bible as your top source for leadership training. There are great leadership books on the shelves of every bookstore, but too often they represent the thinking of mere humans and not the God of the Universe. I trust your leadership journal has become a place of introspection about your leadership and has helped challenge you as a leader.

Sixty-six leadership lessons might seem daunting, so may I suggest we boil them down to three areas, which is exactly what Christ said in Matthew 22:37-40:

> *Jesus replied: "'<u>Love the Lord your God</u> with all your heart and with all your soul and with all your mind.' This is the first and greatest commandment. And the second is like it: '<u>Love your neighbor as yourself.</u>' All the Law and the Prophets hang on these two commandments."*

<u>Love God</u>: The lessons in this book address this idea in 1 Kings, Esther, Job, Isa., Mic., Mal., 1 Cor., Gal., Col., 2 Tim., Jas., 2 Pet., 2 John; <u>love others</u>: lessons from Lev., Num., Deut., Josh., Ruth, 1 Chron., Ezra, Neh., Song of Sol., Joel, Jon., Hab., 2 Cor., 1 Thess., Philem.; and <u>love yourself</u> enough to be a leader of character to personify Christ: lessons from Gen., Ex., Judg., 1 and 2 Sam., 2 Ki., 2 Chron., Ps., Eccles., Jer., Lam., Ezek., Dan., Hos., Amos, Obad., Nah., Hag., Zech., Matt., Mk., Lu., Acts, Rom., Eph., Phil., 2 Thess., 1 Tim., Ti., 1 Pe., 1 Jn., 3 Jn., Jude, Rev.

Over and over again in this book I've challenged you as a leader to abide in Christ (John 15) since this opens the door to become a leader with a passion for God. Abiding in God will slow down your hectic life to reflect on the most important aspect of life—relationship. Your abiding will help you love others (the tapestry where leaders work in the lives of others), and help you check on your heart to keep from becoming a person of hubris, materialism and selfishness. As you learn to love God, your heart will be challenged to live like Christ, and this will translate into a love for those you lead and serve.

Please visit this book's Facebook page and let me know what you think about *Leadership by The Book*. May our wonderful God use you as an example of Godly leadership.

Brent Garrison, Ph.D.

About the Author

Dr. Brent Garrison currently serves as the Vice President of Education with CEO Forum in Colorado Springs, Colorado. Dr. Garrison works with over 50 CEOs around the country who oversee a wide variety of public and private companies, universities and non-profits.

In his 32 years in Christian higher education, Dr. Garrison served as Vice President of External Studies at Moody Bible Institute in Chicago. He also served 10 years as Dean of Students at LeTourneau University and Moody Bible Institute. For 15 years Dr. Garrison served as the President of Arizona Christian University in Phoenix, Arizona.

Some of his teaching experiences include teaching high school sciences; college courses in business and leadership at LeTourneau University (Teacher-of-the-Year Award); courses in Bible and Christian Education through Moody Bible Institute's External Studies Division; graduate courses in Student Development at Briercrest University; and an educational psychology course for Moody Bible Institute's Graduate Division. He also taught overseas as a visiting scholar at Siping Normal University in China and English in a Chinese high school; also lectured at Asian Theological Seminary in Manila, Philippines in church leadership. He co-authored a book on spiritual disciplines with Don Whitney, contributed to *The Inspired Leader: 101 Biblical Reflections for Becoming a Person of Influ*ence, as well as written numerous articles on faith and worldview. Family

Life Radio aired a daily radio program by Dr. Garrison on Church History, *On This Day.*

Dr. Garrison has a doctorate in educational administration, masters in educational administration, undergraduate degree in history and extensive study in Bible/Theology.

Dr. Garrison has been married to Maggi for over 40 years and together they have four grown children and five grandkids. Maggi serves as the director of their Missions Ministry and Women's Ministries at their church and has a graduate degree in library science.

They enjoy traveling—especially visiting missionaries on the field (having visited 40 countries). Brent is a voracious reader, enjoys motorcycle trips (and anything with wheels), golfing and drinking strong coffee.

elevate
publishing

A strategic publisher empowering authors to strengthen their brand.

Visit Elevate Publishing for our latest offerings.
www.elevatepub.com

NO TREES WERE HARMED
IN THE MAKING OF THIS BOOK

OK, so a few
did need to make the ultimate sacrifice.

In order to steward our environment,
we are partnering with *Plant With Purpose*, to plant
a tree for every tree that paid the price for the printing of
this book.

PLANT W TH PURPOSE

www.plantwithpurpose.org

CPSIA information can be obtained
at www.ICGtesting.com
Printed in the USA
FSOW01n1724070316
17627FS

9 781943 425020